军事英语综合教程
An Integrated Course for Military English

主编 陈光明 李欣 田文杰

国防工业出版社
·北京·

内容简介

本书是一本通用军事英语教材,涵盖入伍新训、军校教育、维和行动、部队任职教育、空军装备(军用飞机、空天信息技术装备、防空反导装备)、军事演习、我国国防政策、外国空军简介等内容。本书根据"情境式任务教学模式"编排教学内容和教学活动,通过设计主题读译、视频听说、情境演练,在传授军事相关知识及语言的同时,全方位训练学生的军事英语听、说、读、译等各项技能,培养学生的军事外语素养和国际军事视野。

本书适合作为军队院校,尤其是空军院校的非英语专业学员的教材,也适合高校非英语专业国防生,以及部队参加对外军事交流的官兵使用。

图书在版编目(CIP)数据

军事英语综合教程 / 陈光明,李欣,田文杰主编. —北京:国防工业出版社,2014.8(2017.4 重印)
ISBN 978-7-118-09629-3

Ⅰ.①军… Ⅱ.①陈…②李…③田… Ⅲ.①军事 – 英语 – 教材 Ⅳ.①H31

中国版本图书馆 CIP 数据核字(2014)第 151217 号

※

国防工业出版社出版发行
(北京市海淀区紫竹院南路23号 邮政编码100048)
三河市众誉天成印务有限公司印刷
新华书店经售

*

开本 787×1092 1/16 印张 8 字数 166 千字
2017 年 4 月第 1 版第 5 次印刷 印数 12001—15000 册 定价 38.00 元
(本书如有印装错误,我社负责调换)

国防书店:(010)88540777 发行邮购:(010)88540776
发行传真:(010)88540755 发行业务:(010)88540717

编 委 会

策　划　张　军　王　锋
主　编　陈光明　李　欣　田文杰
副主编　杨　琨　郭　良　付小兰　潘　迪
编　者　刘　燕　郭　婉　谢宇晖　林　蓉　邵轶君　白　岚
　　　　　何丽娜　王　珺　葛　薇　贾新艳　任小红　任　君
　　　　　陈彩霞　杨小双　康鹄伟　秦粉玲　聂潇潇　董于萨
　　　　　丁　凌　何　静　王　珍　杨　敏

前　言

随着我国综合国力的不断增强和对外军事交流活动的日益增加,我军在联合国维和行动、国际人道主义救援、联合军演等方面发挥着越来越重要的作用。因此,军事外语交流能力已成为新型军事人才必需的一项重要技能。军队院校是开展我军军事外语教学的主战场,军校外语教学的军事转型成功与否对我军官兵对外军事交流能力的培养意义重大。为适应空军对外军事交流的需要,有针对性地培养空军军官的军事外语交流能力,特编写本教材。

本教材是一本综合性通用军事英语教材,旨在进行传授军事及语言相关知识的同时,全方位训练学生的军事英语听、说、读、译等各项技能,同时培养学生的军事素养和国际军事视野。教材共分10个单元,内容主要涉及美国空军简介、入伍新训、军校教育、部队任职教育、空军装备(军用飞机、空天信息技术装备、防空反导装备)、军事演习、维和行动、我国国防政策等主题。每个单元分别由"Synopsis"、"Learning Objectives"、"Reading to Know"、"Watching to Speak"、"Scenario Simulation"、"New Words"、"Military Terms"和"Cultural Notes"等部分组成。

本教材编写遵循专门用途英语教学的特点,根据"情境式任务教学模式"编排教学内容、设计教学活动。在内容上,选材紧贴军校学员的生活、未来岗位任职及国际军事交流的实际,兼具知识性、专业性和实用性,语言规范、语料真实。利用文字、图片和视频素材,创设生动立体化的军事英语学习情境。在学习任务设计上,本着以学生为中心,以能力培养为目标的原则,综合考虑学生的认知规律,学习任务的真实性、可行性和有效性,设计难度适当、贴近实际的多样化读、译、听、说等军事英语学习任务,引导学生在"用中学"。教材的编排形式符合学生的学习规律,环环相扣,从阅读输入到视听输入,递进式穿插口语输出任务,让学生感受到学习军事英语的乐趣和实际意义。

本书适合作为军队院校,尤其是空军院校的非英语专业学员的教材,也适合高校非英语专业国防生,以及部队参加对外军事交流的官兵使用。

由于编者水平有限,如有疏漏不当之处,敬请读者斧正。

本书视频资料免费领取联系邮箱为:militaryenglish@163.com

编　者

2014 年 5 月

CONTENTS

Unit 1　The United States Air Force　………………………………………　1

Unit 2　Basic Cadet Training　……………………………………………　14

Unit 3　Military Education　………………………………………………　25

Unit 4　Vocational Training　………………………………………………　35

Unit 5　Military Aircraft　…………………………………………………　46

Unit 6　Information Warfare　……………………………………………　61

Unit 7　Missile Defense　……………………………………………………　73

Unit 8　Red Flag Exercise　………………………………………………　87

Unit 9　UN Peacekeeping　…………………………………………………　99

Unit 10　National Defense　………………………………………………　110

Unit 1　The United States Air Force

> **Synopsis**
>
> Do you want to know the core functions and capabilities of the United States Air Force, which is said the largest and one of the world's most technologically advanced air forces? Unit 1, *The United States Air Force*, introduces the overall information about the U. S. Air Force ranging from mission, history, rank, uniforms as well as training and fitness tests. It gives an account of the strategic function and the decisive force as well as the rapid development of the U. S. Air Force.

Learning Objectives

1. to know about the basic information about the U. S. Air Force
2. to learn to talk about the U. S. Air Force with idiomatic expressions
3. to understand the strategic function of the U. S. Air Force

Part I　Reading to Know

Task 1　Read the text.

The United States Air Force

The United States Air Force (USAF) is the aerial warfare service branch of the United States Armed Forces and one of the seven American uniformed services. The U. S. Air Force is a military service within the Department of the Air Force, one of the three military departments of the Department of Defense. It provides air support to ground troops and aids in the recovery of troops in the field. As of 2012, the service operates 5,484 aircraft, 450 Intercontinetal Ballistic Missiles(ICBMs) and 63 satellites. It has a $140 billion budget with 332,854 active personnel, 185,522 civilian personnel, 71,400 reserve personnel, and 106,700 air guard personnel.

Mission

In general, the United States Air Force shall include aviation forces both combat and service not otherwise assigned. It shall be organized, trained, and equipped primarily for prompt and sustained offensive and defensive air operations. US Code defines the purpose of the USAF as: to preserve the peace and security, and provide for the defense, of the United States, the territories, commonwealths, and possessions, and any areas  occupied by the United States; to support national policy; to implement national objectives; to overcome any nations responsible for aggressive acts that imperil the peace and security of the United States. The stated mission of the USAF today is to "fly, fight, and win in air, space, and cyberspace".

History

The War Department created the first antecedent of the Air Force in 1907, which through a succession of changes of organization, titles, and missions advanced toward eventual separation 40 years later. The U. S. Army Air Force became a separate military service on 18 September 1947, with the implementation of the National Security Act of 1947. The Act created the National Military Establishment (renamed Department of Defense in 1949), which was composed of three subordinate Military Departments, namely the Department of the Army, the Department of the Navy, and a newly created Department of the Air Force. Since 2005, the USAF has placed a strong focus on the improvement of Basic Military Training (BMT). In 2007, the USAF undertook a reduction-in-force. Because of budget constraints, the USAF planned to reduce the service's size from 360,000 active duty personnel to 316,000. In 2009, the USAF released a force structure plan that cuts fighter aircraft and shifts resources to better support nuclear, irregular and information warfare.

Administrative Organization

The Department of the Air Force is one of three military departments within the Department of Defense, and is managed by the civilian Secretary of the Air Force, under the authority, direction, and control of the Secretary of Defense. The senior officials in the Office of the Secretary are the Under Secretary of the Air Force, four Assistant Secretaries of the Air Force and the General Counsel, all of whom are appointed by the President with the advice and consent of the Senate. The senior uniformed leadership in the Air Staff is made up of the Chief of Staff of the Air Force and the Vice Chief of Staff of the Air Force.

Personnel

The classification of any USAF job is the Air Force Specialty Code (AFSC). They range from flight combat operations such as a gunner, to working in a dining facility to ensure that members are properly fed. There are many different jobs in fields such as computer specialties, mechanic specialties, enlisted aircrew, communication systems, cyberspace operations, avionics technicians, medical specialties, civil engineering, public affairs, hospitality, law, drug counseling, mail operations, security forces, and search and rescue specialties.

Rank

USAF rank is divided between enlisted airmen, non-commissioned officers, and commissioned officers, and ranges from the enlisted Airman Basic (E-1) to the commissioned rank of General (O-10). Enlisted promotions are granted based on a combination of test scores, years of experience, and selection board approval while officer promotions are based on time-in-grade and a promotion board. Promotions among enlisted personnel and non-commissioned officers are generally designated by increasing numbers of insignia chevrons. Com-

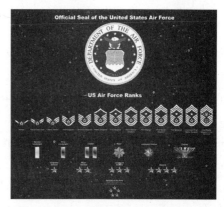

missioned officer rank is designated by bars, oak leaves, a silver eagle, and anywhere from one to four stars (one to five stars in war-time).

Uniforms

The current Service Dress Uniform, which was adopted in 1993 and standardized in 1995, consists of a three-button, pocketless coat, similar to that of a men's "sport jacket" (with silver "U.S." pins on the lapels, with a silver ring surrounding on those of enlisted members), matching trousers, and either a service cap or flight cap, all in Shade 1620, "Air Force Blue" (a darker purplish-blue). This is worn with a light blue shirt (Shade 1550) and Shade 1620 herringbone patterned necktie.

Badges

In addition to basic uniform clothing, various badges are used by the USAF to indicate a job assignment or qualification-level for a given assignment. Badges can also be used as merit-based or service-based awards. Over time, various badges have been discontinued and are no longer distributed. Authorized badges include the Shields of USAF Fire Protection, Security Forces, and the Missile Badge, which is earned after working in a missile system maintenance or operations capacity for at least one year.

Training

All non-prior service enlisted airmen attend Basic Military Training (BMT) at Lackland Air Force Base in San Antonio, Texas for 8 1/2 weeks. The Air Force accepts the basic-training programs of other U.S. military branches in lieu of BMT for airmen who enlist having completed prior service in the U.S. Army, Navy, or Marine Corps. Officers may be commissioned upon graduation from the United States Air Force Academy, upon gradua-  tion from another college or university through the Air Force Reserve Officer Training Corps (AFROTC) program, or through the Air Force Officer Training School (OTS).

Air Force Fitness Test

The US Air Force Fitness Test (AFFT) is designed to test the abdominal circumference, muscular strength/endurance and cardiovascular respiratory fitness of airmen in the USAF. In the AFFT, airmen are given a score based on performance consisting of four components: waist circumference, the sit-up, the push-up, and a 1.5-mile (2.4 km) run. Airmen can potentially earn a score of 100 and a passing score is 75 points.

Culture

The United States Air Force is the largest and one of the world's most technologically advanced air forces. Mark Welsh has called the USAF "a service that prides itself on being fueled by innovations, was born of technology and must stay ahead of the technological curve to be successful". The culture of the United States Air Force is primarily driven by pilots and so the pilots of various aircraft types have driven its priorities over the years.

Task 2 Answer the following questions.

1. What is the stated mission of the USAF today?

2. When and how did the USAF become a separate military service?

3. What senior officials is the Office of the Secretary of the Air Force made up of?

4. How are USAF promotions granted?

5. How are various badges used by the USAF?

6. What is the Basic Military Training (BMT) of the USAF?

Task 3　Complete the following translation tasks.

1. Chinese into English

1）美国空军是美国军队中的空军部分,是美国国防部三大军种之一。
_____

2）美国空军人员分为士兵、士官和军官,军衔设置从列兵到上将。
_____

3）一般情况下,如无另行安排,美国空军包括所有从事作战和维护任务的航空部队。
_____

4）美国空军公布了一项部队结构计划,称其将削减战斗机数量,转而大力支持核战、非常规战和信息战。
_____

5）空军部的高层官员包括部长、副部长、助理部长和总顾问,他们须经参议院举荐并一致通过,由总统任命。
_____

2. English into Chinese

　　The United States Air Force is the largest and one of the world's most technologically advanced air forces. Mark Welsh has called the USAF "a service that prides itself on being fueled by innovations, was born of technology and must stay ahead of the technological curve to be successful". The culture of the United States Air Force is primarily driven by pilots and so the pilots of various aircraft types have driven its priorities over the years.

Task 4　Give an oral presentation in class on the following topics.

1. A Brief Description of the Current Service Dress Uniform of USAF

2. A Brief Introduction to Your Fitness Test

Part II　Watching to Speak

Topic 1　American Airman

Task 1　Watch the video and tell your desk-mate what it is about.

Task 2 Watch the video clip and fill in the blanks.

I'm an American airman. I'm a (1)_____. I have answered (2)_____. My mission is to (3)_____. I am faithful to (4)_____, a tradition of (5)_____ and a legacy of (6)_____.

Task 3 Watch again and tell what American airmen compare themselves to when they pledge to defend the country with their lives.

Task 4 Watch and tick what the American airman will provide to defend the freedom and justice of the United States.

☐ rapid global mobility ☐ great challenge ☐ some obstacles
☐ people's need ☐ air and space ☐ agile combat support
☐ information superiority ☐ defeat ☐ global attack
☐ freedom and justice ☐ virtual enemies ☐ precision engagement

Task 5 Watch the video again and complete the lyrics.

The Airman's Creed

I am an American airman.
I am a _____.
I have answered _____.
I am an American airman.
My mission is to _____.
I am faithful to a proud heritage,
A tradition of _____,
And a legacy of _____.
I am an American airman.
_____ of freedom and justice,

My nation's _____,
It's sentry and avenger.
I defend my country _____.
I am an American airman, wingman, leader, warrior.
I will never leave an airman _____,
I will never _____,
And I will not fail.

Task 6 Talk with your partners about China Air Force creed. You may refer to the following sentence patterns.

I am a... My mission is to... I am faithful to... I defend my country with... I will never..., I will never..., and I will never...

Topic 2 Aviation Career

Task 1 Watch the video clip and tell your desk-mate what it is about.

Task 2 Watch again and tick True (T) or False (F) about the missions of the National Guard helicopter crews.

1. American National Guard helicopter crews' sole mission is to defend the nation's freedom and justice. ☐ T ☐ F
2. American National Guard helicopter crews are engaged in security operations and disaster relief. ☐ T ☐ F
3. American National Guard helicopter crews will not participate in an air assault. ☐ T ☐ F
4. American National Guard helicopter crews may be involved in an emergency medical evacuation. ☐ T ☐ F
5. The helicopter crews might be evacuating civilian victims from a fire. ☐ T ☐ F
6. Every member of Aviation Branch has an important job to do. ☐ T ☐ F

Task 3 Watch the video clip and answer the questions.

What will a pilot practice to be trained into a qualified one?	• to take off and land in the tidy spaces • • •
How can a pilot become a commissioned officer?	•
What is the fastest way to become a helicopter pilot, as early as at the age of 18?	•

Task 4 Watch the video and fill the blanks.

Pilot and crews count on their own aircraft, so they also count on (1) _____ to keep them ready to fly. As a member of the (2) _____, you'll be trained in a critical area of (3) _____ and everything in between. There is a team member who (4) _____ in keeping every part and system (5) _____.

Task 5 Watch again and decide which is the best way to get the training and the education you need if you want to become a helicopter pilot.

Task 6 Talk with your partner about the possible ways of becoming a commissioned officer in China. You may refer to the following phrases and sentence patterns.

  enlisted soldiers   non-commissioned officers   civilians   civilian universities
  basic military units   military academy   cadets   national defense students

  ... *is commissioned. ... take advantage of the officer programs. After... , if you qualify, you can move straight to... It's the best way to... And it's the fastest way to... , even as early as at the age of 18, from high school to ...*

Topic 3   U.S. Air Force

Task 1 Watch the video clip and discuss in groups what it is about.

Task 2 Watch again and fill in the blanks.

Above all, we defend (1) _____.

Above all, we defend (2)_____.

Above all, we are worriers who (3)_____ air, space and cyberspace.

Above all, we are brothers and sisters who (4)_____.

Above all, we (5)_____ before the battle even begins.

Above all, there is nothing our friends (6)_____ more and our enemies (7)_____ more than the (8)_____ of the U.S. Air force.

Above all, we stand ready as the (9)_____ for the 21st century.

Above all, we are the U.S. Air force.

Task 3 Watch the video clip and tell what the U.S. Air Force started with.

Task 4 Watch the video clip and fill in the table about the set-up of the U.S. Air Force.

the courage	• to dream •
the dedication	•
the commitment	•
the sacrifice	•
the cause	• •

Task 5 Watch again and talk with your partner about the history of the establishment as well as the development of China Air Force.

Part III Scenario Simulation

Work in groups. Act out the following scenarios with the language you have learned in this unit.

Scenario 1 The Air Force Academy Recruitment

Instructions: One student acts as a commissioned officer of an Air Force Academy, who is in charge of the recruitment. Two act as graduating high school students enquiring about the career, tasks, training, programs and promotions of the airman.

Scenario 2 A Publicity Film for the Establishment Anniversary of China Air Force

Instructions: You are supposed to design a publicity film (or PPT) for the establishment anniversary of China Air Force. Your work should include at least the history, development, mission, vision, functions, and achievements of China Air Force since its establishment.

New Words

1. antecedent 先驱,前提
2. abdominal 腹部的
3. circumference 周长,全围
4. cardiovascular 心血管的
5. respiratory 呼吸的
6. sit-up 仰卧起坐
7. push-up 俯卧撑
8. innovation 创新,革新
9. prompt 立即的,迅速的
10. sustained 持久的,持续的
11. designate 指派,任命
12. insignia 标志,徽章
13. chevron V 形臂章
14. legacy 传统,遗产
15. valor 英勇,勇猛
16. accountability 义务,责任
17. sentry 哨兵,岗哨
18. avenger 复仇者
19. agile 敏捷的,机敏的
20. superiority 优势,优越性
21. creed 信条,教义
22. aviation 飞行,航空

Military Terms

1. aerial warfare 空战
2. ground troops 地面部队
3. ICBM (Intercontinental Ballistic Missile) 洲际弹道导弹
4. active personnel 现役军人
5. civilian personnel 文职人员
6. reserve personnel 预备役
7. Air National Guard (ANG) 空军国民警卫队
8. Basic Military Training (BMT) 基本军事训练
9. reduction-in-force 裁军
10. fighter aircraft 歼击机,战斗机
11. nuclear warfare 核战争
12. irregular warfare 非常规战
13. information warfare 信息战
14. Secretary of Defense 国防部长
15. Under Secretary 副国务卿,副部长
16. General Counsel 总顾问,法律顾问
17. enlisted airmen 士兵
18. non-commissioned officer 士官
19. commissioned officer 军官
20. service cap 军帽
21. flight cap 飞行帽
22. combat maneuver 战斗机动
23. USAAF (U.S. Army Air Forces) 美国陆军航空队
24. National Security Act 国家安全法案

Cultural Notes

1. Air National Guard(ANG) 空军国民警卫队

The Air National Guard (ANG), also known as the Air Guard, is the air force militia component of each U.S. state. It is, along with the Army National Guard, an element of the state National Guard. The state Air National Guards are under the jurisdiction of the State Governor or equivalent through the office of the State adjutant general. However, if federalized by order of the President of the United States, ANG units become an active part of the United States Air Force. They are jointly administered by the states (or equivalents) and the United States National Guard Bureau.

2. enlisted Airman Basic (E-1) 列兵

It is the lowest enlisted rank in the United States Air Force (USAF), immediately below airman, the pay grade for airman basic is E-1.

US DoD Pay grade	E-1	E-2	E-3	E-4	E-5	E-6	E-7	E-8		E-9		
Title	Airman Basic	Airman	Airman First Class	Senior Airman	Staff Sergeant	Technical Sergeant	Master Sergeant	Senior Master Sergeant'	Chief Master Sergeant'	Command Chief Master Sergeant	Chief Master Sergeant of the Air Force
Abbreviation	AB	Amn	A1C	SrA	SSgt	TSgt	MSgt	SMSgt	CMSgt	CCM	CMSAF
NATO Code	OR-1	OR-2	OR-3	OR-4	OR-5	OR-6	OR-7	OR-8	OR-9	OR-9	OR-9

' The USAF does not have a separate First Sergeant rank; it is instead a duty denoted by a diamond within the upper field.

Pay grade	O-1	O-2	O-3	O-4	O-5	O-6	O-7	O-8	O-9	O-10	Special¹
Title	Second Lieutenant	First Lieutenant	Captain	Major	Lieutenant Colonel	Colonel	Brigadier General	Major General	Lieutenant General	General	General of the Air Force
Abbreviation²	2d Lt	1st Lt	Capt	Maj	Lt Col	Col	Brig Gen	Maj Gen	Lt Gen	Gen	GAF
NATO Code	OF-1	OF-2	OF-3	OF-4	OF-5	OF-6	OF-7	OF-8	OF-9	OF-10	

¹ Awarded during periods of a declared war.
² No periods are used in actual grade abbreviation.

3. commissioned rank of General (O-10) 美国空军上将军衔

In the United States Army, U.S. Air Force, and U.S. Marine Corps, general is a four-star general officer rank, with the pay grade of O-10.

4. United States Air Force Academy (USAFA) 美国空军军官学校

USAFA is a military academy for officer candidates for the United States Air Force. Its campus is located immediately north of Colorado Springs in El Paso County, Colorado, United States. The Academy's stated mission is "to educate, train, and inspire men and women to become officers of character, motivated to lead the United States Air Force in service to our nation." It is the youngest of the five United States service academies, having graduated its first class in 1959. Graduates of the Academy's four-year program receive a Bachelor of Science degree, and are commissioned as second lieutenants in the United States Air Force.

5. Air Force Reserve Officer Training Corps (AFROTC) 空军后备军官训练团

AFROTC is one of the three primary commissioning sources for officers in the United States Air Force, the other two being the United States Air Force Academy (USAFA) and Air Force Officer Training School (OTS). A subordinate command of the Air University within the Air Education and Training Command (AETC), AFROTC is aligned under the Jeanne M. Holm Center for Officer Accessions and Citizen Development at Maxwell AFB, Alabama. AFROTC is the largest and oldest source of commissioned officers for the U.S. Air Force. Its stated mission is to produce quality leaders for the U.S. Air Force.

6. Air Force Officer Training School (AFOTS) 美国空军军官培训学院

AFOTS is a United States Air Force commissioning program located at Maxwell Air Force Base in Montgomery, Alabama. It is the current de facto officer candidate school (OCS) program for the U.S. Air Force, analogous to the OCS programs operated by the other branches of the U.S. armed forces.

Unit 2 Basic Cadet Training

> **Synopsis**
>
> Do you want to know where future Air Force officers and pilots come from and how they are developed into leaders of character in the U. S. ? Unit 2, *Basic Cadet Training*, gives you the exciting and vivid account of a group of basic cadets in the United States Air Force Academy in "Reading to Know" and the United States Military Academy in "Watching to Speak". It illustrates the challenges new cadets face during their grueling basic training and the upper-class cadets charged with leading them.

Learning Objectives

1. to know about the basic cadet training in the military academies in the United States
2. to learn to talk about basic cadet training with idiomatic expressions
3. to understand the significance of basic cadet training

Part I   Reading to Know

Task 1   Read the text.

Basic Cadet Training (BCT) in USAFA

The freshmen have just arrived, fresh off the bus and in total culture shock! The majority are recent high school graduates, tops in their class, but at the Academy they are just the new "average". The Seniors (1 st Class Cadets—"Firsties") are barreling toward graduation and this is their last opportunity to use what they have learned about leadership to train and lead the freshmen. From the science whizzes to the jocks—they must learn to become warriors and by working together as a team!

"In-processing Day"

Dawn breaks on the Colorado foothills. It is June and there is a slight chill yet in the morning air. Over a thousand young people complete their paperwork, bid their loved ones "Goodbye" and board blue Air Force Academy buses that will take them away to basic cadet training. Each arriving "Basic Cadet" has their own reason for being here. Some of them have already attended a year at the Academy's Prep-School to help them ready academically. A smattering had already enlisted in the Air Force and spent time as Airmen on active duty. But most are "Direct Entries".

Every new cadet entering the U. S. Air Force Academy begins basic cadet training (BCT) on his first day. BCT occurs during a six-week period before actual classes begin for a freshman's first year.

The Rigors of BCT

Each of BCT's two phases—one in the cadet area, the other in Jacks Valley—makes its own demands and offers its own rewards. BCT will challenge new cadets physically, mentally and emotionally. Their commitment to themselves, to those close to them will be tested daily. They'll expand their limits and emerge with a deep sense of pride and confidence in their accomplishments and abilities. They'll begin to understand what sets the Academy apart from other colleges and universities.

Basic Cadet Training Part 1 (BCT 1) —"First Beast"

Once aboard the blue bus of the USAFA, the training begins. The basic cadets are now members of the military and it is the job of the upperclassmen to train them and turn them into 4 th Class Cadets, a title the new freshmen will have to earn. The Seniors (1 st Class Cadets — "Firsties"), and Juniors (2 nd Class Cadets — "2-Degrees) descend on the basic cadets with an in-your-face barrage of instructions and orders beginning with remembering and reciting the Seven Basic Responses. This first day and the following days of BCT 1, take place on "The Hill" in the Cadet Area of the Academy. It is a blur of early morning wake-ups, memorizing names, learning military protocol, honor lessons, Air Force heritage, learning to eat meals at attention and prepare for room inspection. They are required to demonstrate their proficiency through physical conditioning training, including drill, rifle-manual competitions, strenuous exercises, running, competitive sports and parades. Here they are broken down as individuals in preparation to be built back up as a team.

Basic Cadet Training Part 2 (BCT 2)— "Second Beast" in Jack Valley

At times, the basic cadets question why they are here and whether they will make it through. And just as they begin to master BCT 1, it is time to begin Basic Cadet Training Part 2 in Jacks Valley, a section of the Academy, an encampment five miles away from the cadet area, near Colorado Springs, Colorado and challenge courses of various kinds. The second phase lasts 18 days and focuses on weapons training, field training and developing stamina.

Under the leadership of a tough new commander and his staff, one senior cadet proves to be the kind of leader who inspires others by leading by example, culminating with running the grueling Assault Course with his basic cadets. His "first boots in— last boots out" drives home the lesson of caring about those you lead.

Basic cadets stay in Jacks Valley will involve many activities, which will push them to their physical limits and build within them self-confidence and confidence in their classmates. They'll also become familiar with small-unit tactics and firearms. After a challenging and rewarding experience in Jacks Valley, BCT training concludes back in the cadet area.

Second Beast ends for the cadets with a trip to the airfield and rides in the soar planes (gliders) and for one lucky basic cadet, a tandem parachute jump.

"Acceptance Day"

The end of BCT and transition into the academic year are marked by the Acceptance Parade. The basic cadets are awarded their fourth-class shoulder boards to recognize completing BCT and to signify their acceptance into the cadet wing. In a ceremony associated with the parade, new fourth-class cadets culminate the intensive BCT core values, honor, ethics and human relations training by taking the Academy Honor Code Oath and pledging to live by its principles. Though the basic cadets have now become Four-Degrees, they are under freshman restrictions, including only walking on certain sections on the courtyard "terrazzo" and in the hallways, only carrying their backpacks in their left hands, and sitting at attention during meals. The restrictions continue until sometime in March when they prove themselves through three days of "Recognition". A day they look forward to with mixed feelings.

"Recognition"

Ready to be relieved of the freshmen restrictions, the Four-Degrees are ready for the physically and mentally grueling series of challenges the upperclassmen have planned for them over the course of three days, known as "Recognition". Through the ordeal, the Four-Degrees learn many important lessons, including how to help and rely on one-another, before they are awarded their Prop and Wings badge signifying their rite of passage into full acceptance as a cadet. They are now free of the restrictions and speak freely with the upperclassmen and are able to wear civilian clothes again for the first time since arriving at the academy.

After the BCT, the school year begins with tough classes, but a variety of interesting majors to pursue. Cadets participate in aeronautics engineering and one group actually participates in building and tracking a working satellite — with cadets traveling to Alaska for the rocket launch. Meanwhile, the football season begins, and the Falcons are eager to earn back the Commander-in-Chief trophy from Navy.

Task 2 Answer the following questions.

1. How long will the basic cadet training last?

2. What are the backgrounds of the new cadets?

3. What are the training subjects in BCT 1?

4. What are the training subjects in BCT 2?

5. What will new cadets do on the "Reception Day"?

6. When will the freshman restrictions be lifted from the new cadets?

Task 3 Complete the following translation tasks.

1. Chinese into English

1) 新学员刚刚入校,强烈的文化冲击让他们不断问自己是否能坚持下去。

2) 少数新学员已经入伍,成为现役空军士兵。

3) 新学员在新训期间将经历身体、心理和情感上的各种挑战。

4) 作为高年级学员,他的"第一个进,最后一个出"的做法明确了上级必须关心下级这个原则。

5) 在新训的最后,新学员被授予肩章,进行宣誓,这标志着他们正式成为学员联队的一员。

2. English into Chinese

Basic cadets stay in Jacks Valley will involve many activities, which will push them to their physical limits and build within them self-confidence and confidence in their classmates. They'll also become familiar with small-unit tactics and firearms. After a challenging and rewarding experience in Jacks Valley, BCT training concludes back in the cadet area.

Task 4 Give an oral presentation in class on the following topics.

1. A Brief Description of the BCT in the USAFA

2. My Basic Cadet Training

Part II Watching to Speak

Topic 1 Reception Day (R-day)

Task 1 Watch the video clip and tell your desk-mate what it is about.

Task 2 Watch, tick the gender of each new cadet and fill in the form with related information.

	male	female	new cadet	sergeant	personal information
Jay					
David					
Rachael					
Ingrid					
Destefand					

Task 3 Watch again and answer the questions.

No.	What do new cadets do on R-day?	What are the adjectives in the video describing R-day?
1		
2		1. _____
3		2. _____
4		3. _____
5		4. Can you think of any other adjectives beside these three? _____
6		

Task 4   What is the purpose of R-day according to Destefand, the senior cadet in charge of the basic cadet training?

Task 5   New cadets should change into uniform on R-day. Watch and tick what the new cadet put in their big blue bag.

☐ socks	☐ raincoats	☐ sweat pants	☐ uniforms
☐ under pants	☐ T-shirts	☐ badges	☐ shoes
☐ quilts	☐ stationeries	☐ shorts	☐ torches

Task 6   Watch the video and fill in the blanks.
The correct format of answering the four responses of new cadets:
_____
_____

Write out the corresponding drilling orders in China's armed forces:

English drilling orders	Chinese drilling orders
turning on a dime	
about face	
right face	
left face	
left, right, left	

Task 7   Talk with your partner about your first day on the military campus. You may refer to the following sentence pattern.

My R-day started with a ... and then... After that, ... With ..., I reached the last stop of R-day, ...

Topic 2   Physical Training in Beast Barrack

Task 1   Watch the video clip and tell your desk-mate what happens and how it is carried out.

Task 2   Watch the video clip and answer the questions.

What is the training item in the video?	
What's Ingrid's feeling about the training?	
What is Jay's feeling about the training?	

Task 3 Watch the video and tick True (T) or False (F) about the rules in the dining hall.

1. The rules about eating are the strictest among all the other rules at West Point. ☐ T ☐ F
2. Foods cannot be passed cross the table. ☐ T ☐ F
3. Foods should be passed from the left to the right. ☐ T ☐ F
4. Before eating, one of the new cadets reports to the senior cadet indicating that they are ready. ☐ T ☐ F
5. Without the permission of the senior cadet, no one will start eating. ☐ T ☐ F
6. To improve efficiency, cadets are asked to eat as quickly as possible. ☐ T ☐ F

Task 4 Watch the video and fill in the blanks about the room inspection.

There's (1) _____ for Ingrid and the other (2) _____ new cadets. "You don't have (3) _____ and the only is to come around and do what you have to do. Ingrid's dorm has to be (4) _____ before she carries on for more training. Those chains should all be pushed to the right. Everything has (5) _____ like the clipboards. (6) _____ go into the right and sandals go to the left. The corner has to be hostile corners trimmed into 45 degree (7) _____. ... It has to be done every (8) _____ before you leave, cause they come in to (9) _____. You can see over here, our checkout list."

Task 5 Watch the video and link the pictures with the corresponding activities.

mountain climber exercises

obstacle courses

endurance tests

Task 6 Talk with your partner about your military training on the military campus. You may refer to the following phrases and sentence patterns.

marching   military martial arts   formation drilling   rock climbing

shooting   turn on a dime   long distance running   tactics

My military training is both ... (adjective) and ... (adjective). The training items are ... During the first few days, ... I feel ... Later we proceed to ... During the last few days, ...

Topic 3 Simulated War

Task 1 Watch the video clip and discuss in your group what it is about.

Task 2 Watch again and fill in the form about the mission of George and his group-mates on the assault course.

what	assault course
where	
why	
equipments	blank ammo; dummy grenades
mission	navigate _____ and _____ the bunker
how	
How does George feel about actual combat?	
result of the mission	☐ accomplished ☐ failed

Task 3 Watch the video clip and answer the following questions.

1. What does Rachael think about the Basic Cadet Training originally and why?

2. What is the training purpose of their mission?

3. What is the mission of Rachael and her partners?

21

4. What are the conditions they face during the mission?

5. What is the result of the mission?

Task 4　Watch again and put the following sentences in order.

　　a) It's "now or never".
　　b) Rachael throws her fourth and final grenade.
　　c) Rachael launches her third grenade at the target.
　　d) Rachael extends two grenades toward enemy obstacle.
　　e) Rachael is out of bullets.
　　f) Now Rachael's out of grenades.
　　g) Dodging enemy fire, Rachael and her partner move in within the range of the bunker.
　　Correct order: _____

Task 5　Watch for a third time and talk with your partner about what you have learned from the mission. You may refer to the following sentence pattern.

　　Mistakes in battle can carry grave consequences. In Rachael's case, I get to know that ...

Part III　Scenario Simulation

　　Work in groups. Act out the following scenarios with the language you have learned in this unit.

Scenario 1　First Day on the Military Campus

　　Instructions: One of three acts as the upper-class cadet. The other two act as new cadets. Your role-play should include reception, rules learning, drilling in your performance.

Scenario 2　War Game

　　Instructions: think of a mission that you and your partner are going to take, for example to take hold of a hill or to blow up an enemy bunker. Design the details during the mission. You may fall into two groups, the red force (the enemy) and the blue force (good guys).

New Words

　　1. whiz 专家;能手
　　2. smattering 一点;少量的

3. barrage 猛烈攻击;齐射式攻击;(语言)像连珠炮似地猛攻
4. encampment 营地
5. grueling 紧张的;极度疲劳的
6. stamina 耐力
7. culminate 达到顶峰
8. trophy 奖杯;纪念品
9. ordeal 严峻的考验
10. rite 仪式
11. dodge 躲避

Military Terms

1. cadet 军校学员
2. assault 攻击
3. small-unit tactics 小单位战术
4. firearm 轻武器
5. Commander-in-Chief 总司令
6. wing (美空军)联队
7. badge 徽章
8. sergeant 军士;中士
9. gear (士兵的)衣服和装备
10. barrack 兵营
11. formation 编队;队形
12. grenade 手榴弹
13. ammo(ammunition) 弹药
14. bunker 掩体
15. sniper 狙击手
16. cover 掩护

Cultural Notes

1. active duty 现役

the same as active service

2. Seven Basic Responses(新生的)七句话标准回答

Seven standard responses that the Basics must recite when responding to their Cadre are:

Yes, Sir/Ma'am.

No, Sir/Ma'am.

No excuse, Sir/Ma'am.

Sir/Ma'am, may I ask a question?

Sir/Ma'am, may I make a statement?

Sir/Ma'am, I do not know.

Sir/Ma'am, I do not understand.

3. military protocol 军事规约

Refers to the norms to which all members of the hierarchy adhere in order to keep the order of the institution. Various aspects of military protocol include calling someone by the correct title and exclusively using their last name. Other things, such as salutation and the proper wearing of a uniform, are also part of military protocol.

4. Honor Code 荣誉制度

The Code is based on a fundamental, positive principle of honesty, respect, fairness, and support. Honor Code is as follows: We will not lie, steal, or cheat, nor tolerate among us anyone who does.

5. Terrazzo 水磨石广场(学员区的主要建筑物围绕一个被称为水磨石广场建造)

It is the large square pavilion that the main buildings in the Cadet Area are set around. The name comes from the fact that the walkways are made of terrazzo tiles, set among a checkerboard of marble strips.

Unit 3 Military Education

> **Synopsis**
>
> Do you want to know some famous military academies in the U. S. ? Do you want to know how cadets there live their way of life and become officers of character? Unit 3, *Military Education*, briefly introduces three military academies — the United States Air Force Academy, the United States Naval Academy and the United States Military Academy. Meanwhile, it presents the development of cadets there from high school graduates to leaders.

Learning Objectives

1. to know the basic information about the military academies in the U. S.
2. to learn to talk about military education with idiomatic expressions.
3. to understand the significance of military education

Part I Reading to Know

Task 1 Read the text.

The United States Air Force Academy

The United States Air Force Academy (*USAFA*) is a military academy for officer candidates for the United States Air Force. Its campus is located immediately north of Colorado Springs, Colorado. The Academy's stated mission is "to educate, train, and inspire men and women to become officers of character, motivated to lead the United States Air Force in service to our nation." It is the youngest of the five United States service academies, having graduated its first class in 1959. Graduates are commissioned as second lieutenants in the United States Air Force. The Academy is also one of the largest tourist attractions in Colorado, attracting more than a million visitors each year.

Admission

Candidates for admission must be excellent on their academic achievement, leadership, athletics and character. They should be at least 17, but less than 23 years of age. In addition, to gain admission, they must also pass a fitness test, undergo a thorough medical examination, and secure a nomination, which usually comes from the member of Congress in  the candidate's home district. Tuition along with room and board are all paid for by the U. S. government and cadets receive a monthly allowance, but they have to serve a number of years of military service after graduation.

The Cadet Wing

The student body of the Academy is known as the Cadet Wing. The cadets are divided into four classes, based on their year in school. They are not referred to as freshmen, sophomores, juniors and seniors, however, but as fourth-, third-, second- and first class cadets, respectively. In the military structure of the Cadet Wing, first class cadets hold the positions of cadet officers, second class cadets act as the cadet non-commissioned officers and third class cadets represent the cadet junior non-commissioned officers.

The Cadet Wing is divided into four groups, often cadet squadrons each. Each cadet squadron consists of about 110 cadets, roughly evenly distributed among the four classes. Selected first-, second- and third-class cadets hold leadership, operational and support jobs at the squadron, group and wing levels. Cadets live, march and eat meals with members of their squadrons. Military training and intramural athletics are conducted by squadron as well.

Educational Program

The program at the Academy is guided by the Air Force's core values of "Integrity First, Service Before Self, and Excellence in All We Do", and based on four "pillars of excellence": military training, academics, athletics and character development. Each of the components of the program is intended to give cadets the skills and knowledge that they will need for success as officers.

Military Training

Cadets' military training occurs throughout their time at the Academy, but is intense during their four summers. The first military experience for new cadets (called "basic cadets") occurs during the six weeks of Basic Cadet Training (BCT), in the summer before their fourth class year. Basic cadets learn military customs and courtesies, proper wear of the uniform, drill and ceremony, and study military knowledge and undergo a rigorous physical training program. During the second half of BCT, basic cadets march to Jacks Valley, where they complete the program in a field encampment environment.

After the first year, cadets have more options for summer military training. Between their fourth and third class years, cadets undergo training in Air Force operations in a deployed environment (called "Global Engagement") and may participate in flying gliders or free-fall parachute training. Cadets also completed Combat Survival Training (CST) program, which includes survival, evasion, and resistance training portions. During their last two summers, cadets may serve as BCT cadre, travel to active duty Air Force bases and participate in a variety of other research, aviation and leadership programs. They may also be able to take courses offered by other military services. During the academic year, all cadets take formal classes in military theory, operations and leadership.

Academics

The academic program has an extensive core curriculum, in which all cadets take required courses in the sciences, engineering, social sciences, humanities, military studies and physical education. All graduates receive a Bachelor of Science degree. Traditionally, the academic program at the Air Force Academy has focused heavily on science and engineering, with the idea that many graduates would be expected to manage complex air, space and information technology systems. As a result, the Academy's engineering programs have traditionally been ranked highly.

Athletics

All cadets at the Academy take part in the school's extensive athletic program. The program is designed to enhance the physical conditioning of all cadets, to develop the physical skills necessary for officership, to teach leadership in a competitive environment and to build character. The primary elements of the athletic program are intercollegiate athletics, intramural athletics, physical education, and the physical fitness tests.

Each semester, cadets must pass two athletic fitness tests: a 2.4-km run to measure aerobic fitness, and a 15-minute, 5-event, physical fitness test consisting of pull-ups, a standing long jump, sit-ups, push-ups and a 550-memter sprint. Failure to pass a fitness test usually results in the cadet being assigned to reconditioning until he can pass the test. Repeated failures can lead to disenrollment.

The Honor Code and Character Education

The Cadet Honor Code is the cornerstone of a cadet's professional training and development. The Honor Code was developed and adopted by the Class of 1959, the first class to graduate from the Academy and has been handed down to every subsequent class. The Code itself is simple: *We will not lie, steal, or cheat, nor tolerate among us anyone who does.*

To reinforce the importance of honor, character and integrity to future officers, cadets are given an extensive character and leadership curriculum. The Academy's Center for Character and Leadership Development provides classroom, seminar, workshop and experiential-based learning programs to all cadets, beginning when they enter Basic Cadet Training and continuing each year through their last semester at the Academy. The Center's programs, when coupled with the Honor Code and Honor System, establish a foundation for the "leaders of character" that the Academy aspires to produce.

Task 2 Answer the following questions.

1. How can candidates be admitted by USAFA?

2. Who hold the positions of the Cadet Wing?

3. What kind of military training do cadets experience between their fourth and third class years?

4. What athletic programs do cadets take part in?

5. What will happen if a cadet fails to pass the fitness test?

6. What is the Honor Code?

Task 3 Complete the following translation tasks.

1. Chinese to English

1) 学员联队分为4个大队,每个大队中有10个学员中队,每个学员中队大约有110名学员。

2) 新生将会学习军人的基本养成与礼仪、着装标准、演习与庆典,学习军事知识,进行严格的体能训练。

3) 第二次是限时体能测试,涵盖引体向上、立定跳远、仰卧起坐、俯卧撑和550米跑五个项目,所有项目必须在 15 分钟内完成。

_____

4) 未通过体能测试的人通常要求重新训练直到他能够通过测试。

_____

5) 为了强化未来军官们对荣誉、品格以及正直品质的重要意识,学校给学员开设了大量的有关培养品格与领导才能的课程。

_____

2. English to Chinese

   Candidates for admission must be excellent on their academic achievement, leadership, athletics and character. They should be at least 17, but less than 23 years of age. In addition, to gain admission, they must also pass a fitness test, undergo a thorough medical examination, and secure a nomination, which usually comes from the member of Congress in the candidate's home district.

Task 4   Give an oral presentation in class on the following topics.

   1. A Brief Introduction to USAFA

   2. A Brief Introduction to the Educational Program in Your University

Part II   Watching to Speak

Topic 1   The United States Air Force Academy

Task 1   Watch the video clip and tell your desk-mate what the strong point of academic experience is in USAFA.

Task 2   What are the cadets encouraged to be in the classroom?

☐ repeaters   ☐ researchers   ☐ listeners   ☐ spongers
☐ problem-solvers   ☐ observers   ☐ lecturers   ☐ thinkers

Task 3   Watch the video and fill in the blanks.

   All our classroom and instruction is based on (1)_____ and relating the instruction and the classroom to (2)_____.

   Our introductory science sequence is a four-year where they start literally on the first week (3)_____, and in the second semester they're (4)_____ and it will end up (5)_____.

These are active facilities when we are doing active research for a variety of organizations throughout the (6)_____,(7)_____ and (8)_____.

Task 4　Watch the video and tick True (T) or False (F).

1. Series of learning and the environment will help cadets become officers of character.
   □ T □ F
2. Personal interactions help to develop the leaders. □ T □ F
3. The academy develops officers of character through limited ways. □ T □ F
4. Academic performance always comes first. □ T □ F
5. When a cadet finds somebody doing things wrong, he will probably point it out.
   □ T □ F
6. Cadets can get access to the opportunities to build their leadership. □ T □ F

Task 5　Watch the video and tick what can be learned about the academy from the trip.

□ stadium　　　　　　　□ classroom learning　　　□ cadets' life
□ eating habits　　　　　□ rules and regulations　　□ features of buildings
□ sponsor　　　　　　　□ location of the academy　□ history of the academy
□ military training and　 □ psychological status　　 □ explanation of Air Force
　college life　　　　　　　of the cadets　　　　　　　program

Task 6　Watch the video and find out what the first-year cadets may confront and what they are expected to do, then fill in the table.

No.	What they may confront	What they are expected to do
1	be tavgth _____	dive to the water all the way
2	have tests on _____	be able to show that they don't care about _____
3	be pushed to _____ they can be	challenge
4	not be appreciated and _____	build relationship with _____
5	have new profound _____	
6	be difficult	
7	no be used to _____	

Task 7　Talk with your partner about your first year in military academy. You may refer to the following sentence pattern.

When I was a freshman, firstly I felt ... about the life here. But later I realized ... I needed to ... So for freshmen, I think it's best to ...

Topic 2　The United States Naval Academy

Task 1　Watch the video clip and tell your desk-mate what the video is about.

Task 2　Watch the video clip again and fill in the table.

Location	· in Annapolis, Maryland, on the shore of Severn River · _____-acre campus
Size	· _____ undergraduates · average class size: _____ — _____ · student-faculty ratio: _____ — _____ · female: _____ · ethic minority: nearly _____
Admission	· the required _____ · test score: _____ scored above 600 on Math SAT 　_____ scored above 600 on verbal · _____ are top students in high school
Academics	· _____ majors

Task 3　Watch the video clip and fill in the table.

midshipmen	· have a _____ study program · be ready for _____ · be in top _____ · most important quality: _____
Laura Martindale	· one of the first women ever chosen to _____ · The academy teaches you _____. When you are out of the Navy, you are going to be _____.
Jaclyn Jordan	· be preparing a career for _____ · wants to be _____

Task 4　Watch the video and fill in the blanks.

　　This is about a (1) _____. This is about a (2) _____. This is about (3) _____, (4) _____, (5) _____, (6) _____ and (7) _____. We're sharing (8) _____, but (9) _____. We have all come here to prepare (10) _____, (11)

31

Task 5 Watch the video and tick True (T) or False (F) about the rules in the dining hall.

1. There are more military than civilian in the faculty. ☐ T ☐ F
2. Their demanding class work is integrated into their military and professional learning experience. ☐ T ☐ F
3. Academic training is a major focus of the academy's academic year. ☐ T ☐ F
4. Midshipmen's summers are fully devoted to professional training. ☐ T ☐ F
5. Every midshipman is given direct hands-on experience. ☐ T ☐ F
6. Only academic and leadership development play important roles in midshipmen's development. ☐ T ☐ F

Task 6 Talk with your partner about your summer experience in troops. You may refer to the following sentence pattern.

In ... summer vacation, cadets are sent to barracks and they can have some hands-on experience in troops. My summer experience in troops is ... Every morning ... Then, ... In the evening, ... I think the hands-on experience teaches me ...

Topic 3 The United States Military Academy

Task 1 Watch the video clip and guess what it is probably for.

Task 2 Watch the video and fill in the blanks.

Unlike other elite colleges or universities, the value of West Point education is (1) _____. When as an army officer, (2) _____, even your everyday decisions affect the lives of others around the world. Both (3) _____ educate cadets in more than (4) _____ majors in liberal arts, (5) _____. They share a level of (6) _____ and (7) _____ you simply can't find anywhere else.

West point graduates are affective (8) _____ with both (9) _____ and grand level perspectives. Our classrooms are windows to the world. And you can learn to execute (10) _____, and experience real-time (11) _____.

Task 3 Watch the video and tick True (T) or False (F).

1. Conformity is the rule No. 1. ☐ T ☐ F
2. Cadets needn't to sacrifice their identities. ☐ T ☐ F

3. To be a leader, you must first try to be a leader in your squadron. ☐ T ☐ F
4. If you are attached to your personal freedom, you need not apply. ☐ T ☐ F
5. Usually cadets can't talk with anybody when walking. ☐ T ☐ F
6. Cadets need study and drill on weekends. ☐ T ☐ F

Task 4 Watch the video and tick True (T) or False (F).

1. Cadets need to work 24 hours a day and 7 days a week for 4 long years learning to be officers. ☐ T ☐ F
2. Cadets' training life is isolated. ☐ T ☐ F
3. Cadets study war in classroom and in war games. ☐ T ☐ F
4. Cadets may have opportunities to experience war in real environment. ☐ T ☐ F
5. After their graduation, they may serve as second lieutenants and be sent to different places to lead soldiers. ☐ T ☐ F

Task 5 Talk with your partner about your training life. You may refer to the following sentence pattern.

... usually comes first. We are supposed to ... every day. Besides, we need to ... ... is strictly forbidden during weekdays. We have to ...

Part III Scenario Simulation

Work in groups. Act out the following scenarios with the language you have learned in this unit.

Scenario 1 Basic Information about Your University

Instructions: One acts as the guide. Two act as high school students. The guide should introduce the university to the students and answer questions from them.

Scenario 2 Plan-designing

Instructions: Think of the main aspects like academic, physical, military and professional development, which you are supposed to complete with your partners, hold a meeting to discuss how to develop these aspects efficiently, and then work out a plan.

New Words

1. intercollegiate 大学间的
2. intramural 校内的
3. aerobic 有氧的
4. sprint 短跑

5. reconditioning 再次训练；重新训练
6. cornerstone 基础；地基

Military Terms

1. second lieutenant 少尉
2. fitness test 体能测试
3. Cadet Wing 学员联队
4. non-commissioned officer 军士；士官
5. junior non-commissioned officer 初级军士；初级士官
6. group 大队
7. squadron 中队
8. Global Engagement 全球作战
9. Cadre （负责训练新兵的）干部
10. midshipman 海军学校学员
11. civilian 文职（教员）

Cultural Notes

1. intercollegiate athletics 校际体育赛事

The Academy's intercollegiate program has 17 men's and 10 women's NCAA sanctioned teams, nicknamed the "Falcons(猎鹰)". Men's teams compete in football, baseball, basketball, ice hockey, cross—country, fencing, golf, gymnastics, indoor and outdoor track, lacrosse, rifle, soccer, swimming and diving, tennis, water polo and wrestling. Women's teams include basketball, cross—country, fencing, gymnastics, indoor and outdoor track, swimming and diving, soccer, tennis and volleyball.

2. SAT (Scholastic Assessment Test) 学术能力评估测验

The SAT is a standardized test widely used for college admissions in the United States. The SAT is owned and published by the College Board, a private, nonprofit organization in the United States. It is developed and administered on behalf of the College Board by the Educational Testing Service. The test is intended to assess a student's readiness for college.

3. NASA (National Aeronautics and Space Administration) 美国国家航空航天局（又称美国国家航空和太空管理局）

It is the agency of the United States government that is responsible for the nation's civilian space program and for aeronautics and aerospace research.

Unit 4 Vocational Training

Synopsis

Do you want to know what kind of training Air Force officers and pilots can have after graduation? Unit 4, *Vocational Training*, introduces you some of the exciting and challenging trainings offered in the United States Air Force. It also illustrates you the training goals, training procedures, and the difficulties the Air Force officers and pilots may encounter during the training.

Learning Objectives

1. to know about some vocational training one can apply for in the U.S. army
2. to learn to talk about some vocational trainings with idiomatic expressions
3. to understand the importance and significance of vocational training

Part I Reading to Know

Task 1 Read the text.

A Glimpse at Some Professional Training in USAF

SERE Training

Survival, Evasion, Resistance, and Escape (SERE) is a program, best known by its military acronym, that provides U.S. military personnel, U.S. Department of Defense civilians, and private military contractors with training in evading capture, survival skills, and the military code of conduct. The majority of trainees at the USAF SERE School are Air Force aircrew members—pilots, navigators, flight engineers, loadmasters, boom operators, gunners, and other crew positions. Additionally, some intelligence officers and life support technicians may also attend. Graduates of the

U. S. Air Force Survival School at Fairchild Air Force base in Washington internalize the Survival, Evasion, Resistance and Escape motto of "Return with Honor."

There are different levels and types of SERE training. Currently there are three levels of training. The SERE Level C Course is usually the one that everyone refers to when discussing training for special operators. Level C is considered to be the hardest of the SERE courses and is quite demanding. Special Forces candidates are required to attend the Level C course as part of their training. The course teaches the student how to evade capture, survival skills during evasion, survival skills during captivity, methods of resistance in captivity, and methods of escape. Other topics such as the military code of conduct are taught as well.

Most of SERE training focuses on survival and evasion. Skills taught include woodcraft and wilderness survival in all types of climate. This includes what is known as emergency first aid, a variant of the battlefield variety, land navigation, camouflage techniques, methods of evasion, communication protocols, and how to make improvised tools. Students spend six days in the Colville and Kanisku National Forests mountains, while the rest of the course is conducted at Fairchild. Students first learn how to handle the psychological and physical stress of survival, after which they learn post-ejection procedures and how to handle parachute landings. They are also instructed in survival medicine. Shelter construction, gathering and cooking food, land navigation methods, evasion and camouflage, signaling and aircraft vectoring are all taught during students' six-day stay in the mountains. After their stint outside, students return to Fairchild and learn about how to behave if they are captured.

Future instructors at SERE are taught by the 66th Training Squadron at Fairchild. This program lasts five and half months. It teaches students how to train aircrew members to survive no matter where they land. They learn several skills, including basic survival, navigation, arctic survival, evasion, desert survival, rough land evacuation, tropics/river survival and coastal survival.

Another course taught at Fairchild's SERE is non-ejection water survival. This teaches aircrew members how to survive if they are in an aircraft without parachutes. This course takes two days to complete. Students learn how to signal rescue aircraft, how to find food and drinkable water, how to use a life raft properly, about the physical components of water survival and dangerous water animals.

USAF Weapons School Training

The mission of the USAF Weapons School is to

teach graduate-level instructor courses, which provide advanced training in weapons and tactics employment to officers of the combat air forces. The Weapons School accomplishes its mission by providing graduate-level, instructor academic and flying courses to USAF Combat Air Forces (CAF). It conducts extensive technical off-station training and is a liaison with CAF units. The USAF Weapons School trains tactical experts and leaders of Airmen skilled in the art of integrated battle-space dominance across the land, air, space and cyber domains. Every six months, the school graduates approximately 100 Weapons Officers and enlisted specialists who are tactical system experts, weapons instructors and leaders of Airmen.

During the course, students receive an average of 400 hours of graduate-level academics and participate in demanding combat training missions. The goal of the course is to train students to be tactical experts in their combat specialty while also learning the art of battle-space dominance; this ability to create such a complete overmatch in combat power in any domain of conflict that adversaries have no choice but to submit or capitulate. Using an integrated approach means that Weapons School graduates are extensively familiar not just with the weapons platform or system they have been trained in through their career path, but also in how all USAF and Department of Defense assets can be employed in concert to achieve synergistic effects.

The Weapons School's squadrons include the Weapons Instructor Courses for the following aircraft and systems: Air Battle Manager, A-10 Thunderbolt II, Lockheed AC-130, B-1 Lancer, B-2 Spirit, B-52 Stratofortress, C-17 Globemaster III, C-130 Hercules, EC-130H Compass Call, F-15C Eagle, F-15E Strike Eagle, F-16 Fighting Falcon, F-22A Raptor, Joint Terminal Attack Controller, Unmanned Aircraft Systems, HH-60 Pave Hawk, MC-130, KC-135 Stratotanker, RC-135 Rivet Joint, Intelligence, Space, ICBM, Cyber, and Support.

Tactical Aircraft Maintenance Training

Every jet fighter in the Air Force has the names of two people on it — the pilot's and the crew chief in charge of making sure the plane is ready to fly at a moment's notice. As a Tactical Aircraft Maintenance specialist, you'll be responsible for ensuring everything from tip to tail is maintained to the most exacting standards. If a repair is needed, you'll either do it yourself or engage a specialist and work with them. At the end of the day, the integrity of the plane and the safety of the pilot rest squarely on your shoulders.

After eight and a half weeks of Basic Military Training, every Airman goes to technical training to learn their career. They will have to be able to accomplish the following tasks after their training.

- Perform scheduled inspections, functional checks and preventive maintenance on tactical aircraft and aircraft-installed equipment.
- Prior to flight, you will inspect and perform various functional checks of the aircraft, as well as ensure that the aircraft has been properly serviced with fuel, hydraulic fluid

and liquid oxygen.
- After flight, you will be responsible for ensuring the aircraft is still in operationally ready condition.
- Maintain and repair all parts of the aircraft, performing general mechanical work as opposed to working on a particular system or subsystem.
- If during any of your inspections a malfunction occurs, you will request, through maintenance control, assistance from the shop concerned (engine, electrician, etc.).

Task 2   Answer the following questions.

1. How many levels does SERE consist of? Which level is the hardest?

2. What skills are taught in the survival and evasion part?

3. Who are trained in the USAF Weapons School?

4. What is the goal of the SERE course?

5. What is the tactical aircraft maintenance specialist responsible for?

6. What should the tactical aircraft maintenance specialist do before flight?

Task 3   Complete the following translation tasks.
1. Chinese into English
1) 教员教授学员如何躲避抓捕,躲避过程中所需的生存技能,被囚时如何生存,如何反抗,以及如何逃脱。

2) 学员们首先学习如何应对生存带来的心理和生理压力,之后他们将学习如何伞降。

3）每六个月都会有大约 100 名武器指挥官和专家从武器学校毕业，他们将会成为战术系统专家、武器指挥官和空军的领导人。

4）空军的每一架喷气战斗机上都刻着两个人的名字——飞行员和——地勤组组长，地勤组组长负责确保飞机接到命令后能够随时起飞。

5）机务维修专家主要负责维护飞机，使飞机的每一个部件都达到维护标准。

2. English into Chinese

The Weapons School accomplishes its mission by providing graduate-level, instructor academic and flying courses to USAF Combat Air Forces (CAF). It conducts extensive technical off-station training and is a liaison with CAF units. The USAF Weapons School trains tactical experts and leaders of Airmen skilled in the art of integrated battle-space dominance across the land, air, space and cyber domains.

Task 4 Give an oral presentation in class on the following topics.

1. A Brief Description of the SERE Training Program

2. My First Gun Shooting Training

Part II Watching to Speak

Topic 1 SERE Training Program

Task 1 Watch the video clip and fill in the missing information.

SERE	
Full name of the program	Survival, _____, _____
Trainee	United States _____
Teaching objective	how to deal _____ that you might get a fewer near or get captured by _____
Teaching schedule	_____ months program
Sergeant Grant's description of SERE	not a career for _____

Task 2 SERE recruits are taught to survive in extreme environments. Watch and tick what kinds of environment are mentioned in the video clip.

☐ desert ☐ rainforest ☐ open ocean ☐ arctic
☐ captive situation ☐ jungle ☐ underground ☐ mountain
☐ tropical area ☐ valley ☐ cave ☐ volcano

Task 3 Watch again and answer the questions.

1. When will the word SERE be remembered?

2. Through what can air man learn to survive anywhere in the world?

Task 4 Write down the things SERE recruits learn in the program.

Basic skills	how to	
Combat skills	how to	_____ without getting detected
Other skills		

Task 5 Watch the video clip and answer the questions.

1. What is called escape and evasion?

2. Why are recruits slowing down and having trouble even building a fire?

3. What is recruit's feeling about the training?

4. Which part is the most challenging to the recruit?

Task 6 Talk with your partner about SERE training program. You may refer to the following sentence pattern.

SERE stands for ... It lasts for ... Recruits are taught to ... Things they learn can be divided into ... First, ... Then, ... Apart from that, ... All in all, SERE ...

Topic 2 Weapons School

Task 1 Watch the video and fill in the blanks about the room inspection.

Well really it's giving them those (1) _____ that are the most (2) _____ they will (3) _____. So if they can solve it here and train, the next time they see this, it might be the (4) _____ work, it's not the (5) _____ that they actually get shot at. 19 squadrons, 22 (6) _____ instructor courses, space, (7) _____ and more, all (8) _____ a rigorous five and half months course. And just like the movies, only the top 1 to 5% of the airmen are (9) _____ to attend, even fewer graduate.

Task 2 Watch the video clip and answer the questions.

What do trainees learn in Weapons School?	• •
When did the school found?	•
How long will the training program last?	•
How many airmen can receive the training?	•
What are needed to get into the training?	• •

Task 3 Watch the video and tick True (T) or False (F) about the facts concerning the Weapons School.

1. Trainees receive classroom teaching and scenario training in the air at the same time.
   ☐ T ☐ F
2. Only 100 men and women considered best of the best in the United Stated Air Force are allowed to train here in the Weapons School. ☐ T ☐ F
3. What they learn in Weapons School is basically how to operate different weapons.
   ☐ T ☐ F
4. No matter how good they are, they will have to put to the tests in Weapons School.
   ☐ T ☐ F
5. In Weapons School, trainees can learn to accurately fire weapons in tense situations, win an air-to-air combat, and coordinate with NATO and coalition forces. ☐ T ☐ F

Task 4 Watch the video and fill in the blanks about the flight training.

Some spent (1) _____ more in the air. We sit day and night trying to think of new (2) _____, the challenge, different ways he'll (3) _____ with his critical thinking skills. But that takes a lot of practice. Cornel Daren Sorenson gave us the (4) _____ at how these pilot students train. Today, it's in this F-15 E (5) _____. Within seconds, off the ground. Seconds after that, about (6) _____ Gs and 15,000 feet above Nellis.

Task 5 Watch again and put the following sentences in order.

a) Complete the strike and on to the next.

b) Within seconds, drop to just 3000 feet above the ground, going about 400 miles an hour.

c) Quickly to work and the first exercise scenario.

d) Within seconds, off the ground.

e) Seconds after that, three and a half Gs and 15,000 feet above Nellis.

f) Identify the hostiles and friendlies and assess the situation.

g) We hear a strike call over the radio.

Correct order: _____

Task 6 Watch for a third time and retell the flight training in your own words.

Topic 3 Tactical Aircraft Maintenance Training

Task 1 Watch the video and tick True (T) or False (F) about tactical aircraft maintenance training.

1. Everything the aircraft needs to function properly is what you are in charge of.
   ☐ T ☐ F
2. Students will only learn light control, landing gears and fuel systems. ☐ T ☐ F
3. It's only 30% classroom time and 70% hands-on. ☐ T ☐ F
4. Instructor says students get nervous when they get into the blocks of training.
   ☐ T ☐ F
5. Students cannot swing the landing gear but can do operational checks. ☐ T ☐ F

Task 2 Watch the video and fill in the blanks about tactical aircraft maintenance training.

It's intimidating knowing that the actual life of a pilot is in your hands, but that's what we're here for. (1)_____ the aircraft needs to (2)_____ properly is what you are in charge of. You have to make sure this aircraft is (3)_____ at a moment's notice. What you learn in tactical aircraft maintenance is the base jockey of the jet, learning how to be a (4)_____. You (5)_____ by teaching them aircraft (6)_____. Everything from hydraulics, light control, landing gear, engine and (7)_____. And from there we go in to (8)_____ tasks.

Task 3   Watch again and answer the questions.

Speaker	What do they say about the training?	What are the adjectives they use in the video describing the training?
Instructor		
Trainee		

Task 4   Tactical aircraft maintenance trainees actually have a variety of choices in their future. Watch and tick what are their options.

☐ attend higher lever training afterwards	☐ go directly to maintain commercial aircraft
☐ be a instructor after working on the jet for 10 years	☐ _____
☐ _____	☐ learn another related major
☐ work on the jet for 12 years and switch to other position	☐ _____

Task 5   Talk with your partner about your major. You may refer to the following sentence pattern.

  I majored in ... Its main goal is to... What you are in charge of is ... It's ... knowing... What you learn in ... is/are... it's ... classroom time and ... hands-on. I found the major ... and I am ... to...

Part III   Scenario Simulation

Work in groups. Act out the following scenarios with the language you have learned in this unit.

Scenario 1　Interview

Instructions: One of two acts as the interviewer. Two act as applicants for the USAF Weapons School. You should include requiring the basic information of the applicants, introducing the training program to the applicants. The applicants should pay attention to their attitude.

Scenario 2　SERE Simulation

Instructions: Work in team to simulate the situation of getting away from the downed aircraft and try to survive in the forest and evade enemy detection. Think of the difficulties you might come across and come up with solutions. Discuss with your teammates and decide your best option.

New Words

1. captivity 被俘;囚禁;束缚
2. camouflage 伪装;掩饰
3. protocol 协议
4. improvised 简易的
5. liaison 联络;联络人
6. integrity 完整;完整性
7. malfunction 故障;功能障碍
8. alien 相异的;异己的;不相容的
9. cutting-edge 最前沿的
10. rigorous 严格的; 枯燥的
11. coalition 结合体;联合;同盟
12. hostiles and friendlies 敌人和友军
13. gear 装置
14. hydraulics 液压系统

Military Terms

1. deployment 部署;调度
2. squadron 中队;飞行中队
3. intelligence 情报;情报机构
4. cockpit 驾驶员座舱
5. crew chief 地勤组组长
6. NATO(North Atlantic Treaty Organization)北大西洋公约组织

Cultural Notes

1. F-15 E strike eagle F-15 鹰式战斗机

F-15E Strike Eagle is an American all-weather multirole fighter, derived from the McDonnell Douglas F-15 Eagle. The F-15E was designed in the 1980s for long-range, high speed interdiction without relying on escort or electronic warfare aircraft. United States Air Force (USAF) F-15E Strike Eagles can be distinguished from other U.S. Eagle variants by darker camouflage and conformal fuel tanks mounted along the engine intakes.

2. (three and a half) Gs 重力加速度

G stands for g-force, a measurement of acceleration felt as weight.

3. military code of conduct 美军行为准则

The Code of the U.S. Fighting Force is a code of conduct that is an "ethical guide" and a United States Department of Defense directive consisting of six articles to members of the United States Armed Forces, addressing how American military personnel in combat should act when they must "evade capture, resist while a prisoner or escape from the enemy."

4. Nellis Air Force Base (Nellis AFB) 内里斯空军基地

Nellis Air Force Base is a southern Nevada installation with military schools and more squadrons than any other USAF base. Nellis is the airbase for air combat exercises such as Red Flag and close air support exercises such as Green Flag-West flown in "Military Operations Area (MOA) airspace" associated with the nearby Nevada Test and Training Range (NTTR).

Unit 5　Military Aircraft

> **Synopsis**
>
> As a cadet in the Air Force, you surely are curious about the blue yet mysterious sky, and form a special interest in the man-made wonder flying in it-aircraft. How much do you know about the sophisticated air vehicle? Unit 5, *Military Aircraft*, answers your curiosity and tells you different types of military aircraft plus their features. With various designing purposes, they can work under different conditions and commit missions respectively.

Learning Objectives

1. to know about different types of military aircraft
2. to learn to describe the features of military aircraft with idiomatic expressions
3. to understand the advanced technology in military aircraft

Part I　Reading to Know

Task 1　Read the text.

Military Aircraft

A military aircraft is any fixed-wing or rotary-wing aircraft that is operated by a legal or insurrectionary armed service of any type. Military aircraft can be either combat or non-combat:

Combat aircraft are aircraft designed to destroy enemy equipment using their own armament. Combat aircraft are normally developed and procured only by military forces.

Non-combat aircraft are aircraft not designed for combat as their primary function, but may carry weapons for self-defense. These mainly operate in support roles, and may be developed by either military forces or civilian organizations.

Combat Aircraft

Combat aircraft, or "warplanes", are divided broadly into multi-role, fighters, bombers and attackers, with several variations between them, including fighter-bombers, ground-attack aircraft. Also included among combat aircraft are long-range maritime patrol aircraft that are often equipped to attack with anti-ship missiles and anti-submarine weapons.

Fighter Aircraft

The main role of fighters is destroying enemy aircraft in air-to-air combat, offensive or defensive. Many are fast and highly maneuverable. Escorting bombers or other aircraft is also a common task. They are capable of carrying a variety of weapons, including machine guns, cannons, rockets and guided missiles. Many modern fighters can attack enemy fighters from a great distance, before the enemy even sees them.

A MiG-29 firing an air-to-air missile

Bomber Aircraft

Bombers are normally larger, heavier, and less maneuverable than fighter aircraft. They are capable of carrying large payloads of bombs. Bombers are used almost exclusively for ground attacks and not fast or agile enough to take on enemy fighters head-to-head. A few have a single engine and require one pilot to operate and others have two or more engines and require crews of two or more. A limited number of bombers, such as the B-2 Spirit, have stealth capabilities that keep them from being detected by enemy radar.

A USAAF B-29 Superfortress

Attack Aircraft

Attack aircraft can be used to provide support for friendly ground troops. Some are able to carry conventional or nuclear weapons far behind enemy lines to strike priority ground targets. Attack helicopters attack enemy armor and provide close air support for ground troops.

In modern air forces, the distinction between bombers, fighter-bombers, and attack aircraft has become blurred. Many attack aircraft, even ones that look like fighters, are optimized to drop bombs, with very little ability to engage in aerial combat. Indeed, the design qualities that make an effective low-level attack aircraft make for a distinctly inferior air superiority fighter, and vice versa. Perhaps the most meaningful distinction is that a bomber is generally a long-range aircraft capable of striking targets deep within enemy territory, whereas fighter bombers and attack aircraft are limited to "theater" missions in and around the immediate area of battle-

An A-10 Thunderbolt II firing an AGM-65

field combat. Even that distinction is muddied by the availability of aerial refueling, which greatly increases the potential radius of combat operations.

Multirole Combat Aircraft

A F-15E Strike Eagle dropping a PGB

Many combat aircraft today have a multirole ability. Normally only applying to fixed-wing aircraft, this term signifies that the plane in question can be a fighter or a bomber, depending on what the mission calls for.

Some fighter aircraft, such as the F-16 Fighting Falcon, are mostly used as "bomb trucks", despite being designed for aerial combat.

Non-combat Aircraft

Non-combat roles of military aircraft include search and rescue, reconnaissance, observation/surveillance, Airborne Early Warning and Control, transport, training, and aerial refueling.

Many civil aircraft, both fixed wing and rotary wing, have been produced in separate models for military use, such as the civilian Douglas DC-3 airliner, which became the military C-47 Skytrain, and British "Dakota" transport planes, and decades later, the USAF's AC-47 aerial gunships. Even the fabric-covered two-seat Piper J3 Cub had a military version. Gliders and balloons have also been used as military aircraft; for example, balloons were used for observation during the American Civil War and during World War I, and military gliders were used during World War II to deliver ground troops in airborne assaults.

Military Transport Aircraft

Transport Junkers Ju 52

Military transport (logistics) aircraft are primarily used to transport troops and war supplies. Cargo can be attached to pallets, which are easily loaded, secured for flight, and quickly unloaded for delivery. Cargo also may be discharged from flying aircraft on parachutes, eliminating the need for landing. Also included in this category are aerial tankers; these planes can refuel other aircraft while in flight. Calling a military aircraft a "cargo plane" is incorrect, because military transport planes also carry paratroopers and other soldiers.

Airborne Early Warning and Control

An Airborne Early Warning and Control (AEW&C) system is an airborne radar system designed to detect aircraft, ships and vehicles at long ranges and control and command the battle space in an air engagement by directing fighter and attack aircraft strikes. AEW&C units are also used to carry out surveillance, including over ground targets and frequently perform C2BM (command and control, battle management) functions similar to an Airport Traffic Controller given military command over other forces. Used at a high altitude, the radars on the aircraft allow the operators to distinguish between friendly and hostile aircraft hundreds of miles away.

A USAF E-3 Sentry

AEW&C aircraft are used for both defensive and offensive air operations, and are to the NATO and USA forces trained or integrated Air Forces what the Command Information Center is to a Navy Warship, plus a highly mobile and powerful radar platform. The system is used offensively to direct fighters to their target locations, and defensively in order to counterattacks by enemy forces, both air and ground. So useful is the advantage of command and control from a high altitude, the United States Navy operates AEW&C aircraft off its Supercarriers to augment and protect its carrier Command Information Centers (CICs).

AEW&C is also known by the older terms "airborne early warning" (AEW) and "airborne warning and control system" (AWACS) although AWACS is the name of a specific system currently used by NATO and the USAF and is often used in error to describe similar systems.

Reconnaissance and Surveillance Aircraft

Reconnaissance aircraft are primarily used to gather intelligence. They are equipped with cameras and other sensors. These aircraft may be specially designed or may be modified from a basic fighter or bomber type. This role is increasingly being filled by satellites and unmanned aerial vehicles (UAVs).

A Raytheon Sentinel with a radar pod

Surveillance and observation aircraft use radar and other sensors for battlefield surveillance, airspace surveillance, maritime patrol and artillery spotting. They include modified civil aircraft designs, moored balloons and UAVs.

Experimental Aircraft

Experimental aircraft are designed in order to test advanced aerodynamic, structural, avionic, or propulsion concepts. These are usually well instrumented, with performance data telemetered on radio-frequency data links to ground stations located at the test ranges where they are flown.

Task 2　Answer the following questions.

1. What are the two major types of military aircraft?

2. Can these two types both developed by civilian organizations?

3. Compare fighters and bombers with respect to their size, weight and speed.

4. Which aircraft can refuel other aircraft while in flight?

5. How does the AEW&C system work both offensively and defensively?

6. Which aircraft have the same role as that of satellites and UAVs? What are they equipped with?

Task 3　Write out the corresponding translation of the following aircraft.

English	Chinese
fighter aircraft	
bomber aircraft	
attack aircraft	
electronic warfare aircraft	
maritime patrol aircraft	
multirole combat aircraft	
military transport aircraft	
airborne early warning and control	
reconnaissance and surveillance aircraft	
experimental aircraft	

Task 4　Complete the following translation tasks.

1. Chinese into English

1) 轰炸机几乎完全用于地面攻击，在与敌军战斗机迎面作战时速度不快，也不够灵活。

2) 攻击机可以用来为友军地面部队提供支援。有些攻击机能够携带常规武器或核武器，深入敌方腹地打击地面目标。

3) 军用飞机的非战斗功能包括搜救、侦察、观察/监视、空中预警与控制、运输、训练及空中加油。

4)机载预警与控制系统的设计目的在于对飞机、船舶及车辆等进行远程监测,在空战中通过指挥战斗机从而指控整个空战空间。

5)正如指挥信息中心对于海军战舰的意义一样,空中预警与控制飞机对于北约及美军部队同样至关重要。

2. English into Chinese

In modern air forces, the distinction between bombers, fighter-bombers, and attack aircraft has become quite blurred. Many attack aircraft, even ones that look like fighters, are optimized so as to not capable of engaging in aerial combat. Perhaps the most meaningful distinction lies in that a bomber is generally a long-range aircraft capable of striking targets deep within enemy territory, whereas fighter bombers and attack aircraft are limited to "theater" missions in and around the immediate area of battlefield combat.

Task 5 Give an oral presentation in class on the following topics.

1. Give a brief introduction to the major types of military aircraft. Which one are you mostly interested in? Then say more about it specially.

2. Do some research and briefly introduce a Chinese military aircraft.

Part II Watching to Speak

Topic 1 F-22 Raptor

Task 1 Watch the video clip and describe F-22 Raptor to your desk-mate.

Task 2 Watch the video and tick True (T) or False (F) about the infor-

mation related to F-22.

1. Unlike F-117, the Raptor is very fast, reaching nearly twice the speed of sound.
   □ T □ F
2. F-22 has a secret engine advance called supercruise that maintain subsonic speed by using an afterburner. □ T □ F
3. The Raptor was built to actually maneuver at low altitude. □ T □ F

Task 3 Watch the video clip again and tick the information mentioned about F-22.

□ has two powerful launchers	□ has two powerful engines
□ has a secret engine	□ has a secret engine advance
□ has a theoretical maneuver altitude above 50,000 feet	□ has an actual maneuver altitude above 50,000 feet

Task 4 Watch the video and fill in the blanks.

The Raptor is one last trick up its sleeve, (1) _____. Inspired by the Harrier Jump Jet, it can (2) _____ from it engines' up and down. It can take off (3) _____ or (4) _____, but the system radically improves its (5) _____.

The (6) _____ of the Raptor, cause an opportunity to make it turn a lot quicker and continue to be able to basically point your nose. In a regular type of a basic (7) _____ he who gets its nose in the (8) _____ first wins the fight, so with this actual (9) _____ we can really turn the airplane and essentially (10) _____ twice as better as other airplanes.

Task 5 Talk with your partner about features of F-22. You may refer to the following sentence pattern.

Unlike ..., the Raptor is ... It has ... that produce ... It also has ... The Raptor was built to ... Inspired by ..., it can ...

Topic 2 A-10 Thunderbolt II

Task 1 Watch the video clip and describe A-10 Thunderbolt II to your desk-mate.

Task 2 Watch the video clip again and fill in the blanks.

  The A-10 Thunderbolt II, better known as the Warthog, is one of the artist-looking (1) _____ in the world. Projecting from its front nose is a 30 millimeter cannon specially designed to (2) _____. This weapon, the GAU-8 Gatling gun, fires 50 rounds depleted uranium projectiles (3) _____. The A-10 was designed specifically to (4) _____. Moving at hundreds of miles an hour, fast strike fighter find nearly impossible to (5) _____ such as tanks. And tanks with so heavily armored that require (6) _____ to eliminate.

Task 3 Watch the video again and link the information with the corresponding wars.

The Gulf War	is a war in which small arms fire shot down many expensive fighter bombers
	is a war in which Warthogs flew 8,100 sorties
The Vietnam War	influenced the design of the A-10
	witnessed the use of the A-10
	happened in 1991

Task 4 Watch the video clip again and answer the questions.

 1. What kind of bombs can A-10 carry?

 2. What will help A-10 to defend itself from enemy fighters?

 3. What kind of characteristic does A-10 have in order to extend its range?

 4. What kind of missions does A-10 not commit?

Task 5 Talk with your partner about features of A-10. You may refer to the following sentence pattern.

The A-10 *Thunderbolt II*, *better known as . . . , is one of . . . The A-10 was designed specifically to . . . The A-10, although . . . , is . . . The A-10's unique design came about in part as a result of . . . The A-10 can carry a wide variety of . . . including . . . A standard weapon of the A-10 is . . .*

Topic 3 B-2 Spirit

Task 1 Watch the video clip and discuss in your group what it is about.

Task 2 Watch the video clip again and use the sentences you heard in the clip to illustrate the following items.

RAM	· _____
stealth design	· which makes it _____ _____
reduce signature	· It has _____ signature and _____ signature.

Task 3 Watch the video clip. You may feel confused about the weapons carried by B-2. Answer the following questions with the information you heard and you will figure it out clearly.

What kind of payload does the B-2 carry?	
What conventional weapons does the B-2 carry?	
How many JDAMs and bombs can the B-2 carry respectively?	

Task 4 Watch the video clip again and fill in the blanks.

And its weapons get smaller (1) _____ to carry more and more. What's the means to have sixteen JDAMs in the (2) _____. What the B-2 carries is sixteen 2,000 pound bombs they can all be directed precisely hit a target through (3) _____. They can also be targeted (4) _____, that means they don't have to drop the bombs on one target (5) _____, they can drop them literally on after sixteen different aim points in the same mission. It's a (6) _____ and (7) _____ instrument.

Task 5 Describe the stealth technology of B-2 to your desk-mate. You may refer to the following sentence pattern.

To achieve... , the B-2 relies heavily on ... But other factors also come into play. It gets its stealth design which... It's amazing that... It also...

Topic 4 Global Hawk

Task 1 Watch the video clip and discuss in your group what it is about.

Task 2 Watch the video again and link the following information.

	can travel	40,000 square miles in a single day
The Global Hawk	can survey	60,000 feet
	has an operational altitude of	125,000 nautical miles

Task 3 Watch the video clip for a third time, tick True (T) or False (F) and correct the false statements.

1. Speed and stealth of the Global Hawk is quite impressive. ☐ T ☐ F
2. Global Hawk is a purely reconnaissance aircraft. ☐ T ☐ F
3. Global Hawk doesn't carry any fire power. ☐ T ☐ F

Task 4 Watch the video and fill in the blanks.

The (1) _____ can see at night and through (2) _____ or even in (3) _____. An ability with many (4) _____, the cost of Global Hawk put it out of reach for all but the most (5) _____. But with that cost comes an amazing (6) _____, (7) _____ and a wide array of (8) _____.

Task 5 Discuss in your group about the features of the Global Hawk. You may refer to the following sentence pattern.

Taking the technology of ..., the Global Hawk is literally on top of the world. A single Global Hawk can ... This is only possible because ...

Topic 5 AWACS (Airborne Warning and Control System)

Task 1 Watch the video clip and discuss in your group what it is about.

Task 2 Watch the video clip again and fill in the blanks.

The E-3 Sentry, also known as the Airborne Warning and Control System or AWACS, looks like your typically airplane, except for a large (1) _____ that sits 11 feet above the back of the plane. With that radar, the AWACS provides all-weather (2) _____, (3) _____, (4) _____ and (5) _____ needed by US and (6) _____ allied air commanders. The passenger compartment is filled with (7) _____ equipment that can (8) _____ aircraft in all altitudes, both in the ocean and even direct the allied aircraft against enemy (9) _____.

Task 3 Watch the video clip for a third time and write out the English words of the following terms.

Chinese	English
E-3 预警机	
雷达天线罩	

(续)

Chinese	English
全天候的	
监视	
联合的,同盟的	
隔间,车厢	
侦察并追踪	

Task 4　Watch the video clip and answer the following questions.

What is the core of the AWACS?	
What kind of mission will the personnel on AWACS perform?	
What does a typical crew of AWACS include?	

Task 5　Discuss in your group about the features of AWACS. You may refer to the following sentence pattern.

The ..., also known as ... or ..., looks like ..., except for ... With that ..., the AWACS provides ... needed by ... Success in ... depends on ... ... is at the core of ..., providing... A typical crew includes ...

Part III Scenario Simulation

Work in groups. Act out the following scenarios with the language you have learned in this unit.

Scenario 1　A Visit to Aircraft Models

Instructions: One of two acts as a senior cadet in our university. The other one acts as a new cadet. The former guides the latter to visit the aircraft models landed on the grass in front of the school library. Make up a conversation about the special models. You should consult some sources for relevant information.

Scenario 2　Role Play

Suppose you are a military aircraft expert. You and your research team have invented a new type of aircraft. Hold a press conference, deliver a speech about your new invention, and get ready to answer questions from the journalists. Roles needed: one spokesman, several journalists.

New Words

1. rotary 旋转的
2. insurrectionary 暴动的
3. armament 武器装备
4. armor 装甲
5. maneuverable 机动的
6. maritime 海的
7. airborne 机载的
8. reconnaissance and surveillance aircraft 侦察机
9. predecessor 前身,前辈,前任
10. thrust 推力,拉力
11. supercruise 超声速巡航
12. afterburner 加力燃烧室
13. thrust vectoring 矢量推力
14. vertically 垂直地
15. hover （飞行器）在目标上空盘旋
16. maneuverability 机动性
17. sortie 出击,突围
18. devastating 毁灭性的
19. refueling receptacle 加油容器
20. impunity 不受惩罚或伤害
21. classified 机密的
22. infrared 红外线的
23. acoustic 声音的,声学的
24. signature 性能,特性
25. spectrum 谱,光谱,频谱
26. string 连发弹数
27. flexible 灵活的,机动的
28. unmanned 无人的
29. nautical 海上的,航海的
30. survey 测量,勘测
31. sensor 传感器,遥感器

32. civilian 民用的

33. endurance 续航力,耐航性

34. stealth 隐身

35. array 一系列

36. sophisticated 先进的,尖端的

37. dome 整流罩,圆顶

38. all-weather 全天候

39. compartment 室,舱

40. deploy 部署,调动

41. navigator 领航员

Military Terms

1. PGB power guided bomb 动力制导炸弹
2. Harrier Jump Jet "鹞"式垂直起降飞机
3. GAU-8 "复仇者"机炮
4. Gatling gun "加特林"机枪
5. depleted uranium projectile 贫铀弹
6. Maverick "小牛"空对地导弹
7. anti-aircraft 防空用的
8. Sidewinder "响尾蛇"空对空导弹
9. payload (导弹等武器的)有效载荷
10. bomb bay 炸弹舱
11. operation group 作战大队
12. Air Control Wing 空中控制联队

Cultural Notes

1. strike aircraft & strike fighter 攻击机(强击机)

"Strike aircraft" is an alternative term for a ground-attack aircraft. Whereas in current military parlance, a strike fighter is a multirole combat aircraft designed to operate primarily in the air-to-surface attack role while also incorporating certain performance characteristics of a fighter aircraft. As a category, it is distinct from fighter-bombers. Examples of contemporary American strike fighters are the McDonnell Douglas F-15E Strike Eagle, Boeing F/A-18E/F Super Hornet, and Lockheed Martin F-35 Lightning II.

2. GAU-8 Avenger GAU-8/A 复仇者机炮

The General Electric GAU-8/A Avenger is a 30 mm hydraulically driven seven-barrel Gatling-type cannon that is typically mounted to the United States Air Force's Fairchild Republic A-10 Thunderbolt II. Designed specifically for the anti-tank role, the Avenger delivers very powerful rounds at a high rate of fire. The GAU-8/A is also mounted to the Goalkeeper CIWS.

3. Gatling gun 加特林机枪

The Gatling gun is one of the best-known early rapid-fire weapons and a forerunner of the modern machine gun. Its operation centered on a cyclic multi-barrel design which facilitated cooling and synchronized the firing/reloading sequence. Each barrel fired a single shot when it reached a certain point in the cycle, after which it ejected the spent cartridge, loaded a new round, and in the process, cooled down somewhat. This configuration allowed higher rates of fire to be achieved without the barrel overheating.

4. AGM-65 Maverick missile AGM-65 "小牛"空对地导弹

It is an air-to-surface tactical missile (AGM) designed for close air support. The most widely produced precision-guided missile in the Western world, it is effective against a wide range of tactical targets, including armor, air defenses, ships, ground transportation and fuel storage facilities.

5. The AIM-9 Sidewinder AIM-9"响尾蛇"空对空导弹

It is a short-range air-to-air missile developed by the United States Navy in the 1950s. The majority of Sidewinder variants utilize infrared homing for guidance; the AIM-9C variant used semi-active radar homing and served as the basis of the AGM-122 Sidearm anti-radar missile. The Sidewinder is the most widely used missile in the West. The AIM-9 is one of the oldest, least expensive, and most successful air-to-air missiles, with an estimated 270 aircraft kills in its history of use.

6. stealth technology 隐身技术

Also termed LO technology (low observable technology). It is a sub-discipline of military tactics and passive electronic countermeasures, which cover a range of techniques used with personnel, aircraft, ships, submarines, missiles and satellites to make them less visible (ideally invisible) to radar, infrared, sonar and other detection methods. It corresponds to camouflage for these parts of the electromagnetic spectrum.

7. radar-absorbet material(RAM) 雷达吸波材料

Radar-absorbent material, is a class of materials used in stealth technology to disguise a vehicle or structure from radar detection. A common misunderstanding is that RAM makes an object invisible to radar. A radar-absorbent material can significantly reduce an object's radar cross-section in specific radar frequencies, but it does not result in "invisibility" on any frequency. Bad weather may contribute to deficiencies in stealth capability.

8. Joint Direct Attack Munition (JDAM) 联合制导攻击武器

It is a guidance kit that converts unguided bombs, or "dumb bombs" into all-weather "smart" munitions. JDAM-equipped bombs are guided by an integrated inertial guidance system coupled to a Global Positioning System (GPS) receiver, giving them a published range of up to 15 nautical miles (28 km). When installed on a bomb, the JDAM kit is given a GBU (Guided Bomb Unit) nomenclature, superseding the Mark 80 or BLU (Bomb, Live Unit) nomenclature of the bomb to which it is attached.

Unit 6　Information Warfare

Synopsis

Do you want to know how information is transmitted and applied in modern warfare? Unit 6, *Information Warfare*, gives a brief introduction to the Global Positioning System (GPS) and the Defense Satellite Communication System (DSCS) by which information is acquired and transmitted. Effective protection against cyber attacks by securing information and networks is also a major issue discussed in this chapter.

Learning Objectives

1. to know about the GPS and how it works to give location information
2. to learn to talk about DSCS with idiomatic expressions
3. to understand the importance of information security in modern warfare

Part I　Reading to Know

Task 1　Read the text.

Introduction

Modern warfare is characterized by rapid and successful acquisition and application of information. Not so long ago, satellites were exotic, top-secret devices used primarily in a military capacity, for activities such as navigation and espionage. Now they're an essential part of our daily lives. We see and recognize their use in weather reports. We watch television signals transmitted by them. We have GPS receivers in our cars and smart phones to help us find our way to any destination. And at the same time we also marvel at the amazing large amount of information acquired on the network-centric communication systems. Now let's see what they can do and how they work.

GPS

The Global Positioning System is vast, expensive and involves a lot of technical ingenuity, but the fundamental concepts at work are quite simple and intuitive.

When people talk about "a GPS", they usually mean a GPS receiver. The Global Positioning System (GPS) is actually a constellation of 27 Earth-orbiting satellites (24 in operation and three extras in case one fails). The U.S. military developed and implemented this satellite network as a military navigation system, but soon opened it up to everybody else.

Each of these 3,000- to 4,000-pound solar-powered satellites circles the globe at about 12,000 miles (19,300 km), making two complete rotations every day. The orbits are arranged so that at any time, anywhere on Earth, there are at least four satellites "visible" in the sky.

A GPS receiver's job is to locate four or more of these satellites, figure out the distance to each, and use this information to deduce its own location. This operation is based on a simple mathematical principle called trilateration.

In order to make the calculation, then, the GPS receiver has to know two things:
- the location of at least three satellites above you
- the distance between you and each of those satellites

The GPS receiver figures both of these things out by analyzing high-frequency, low-power radio signals from the GPS satellites. Better units have multiple receivers, so they can pick up signals from several satellites simultaneously.

A standard GPS receiver will not only place you on a map at any particular location, but will also trace your path across a map as you move. If you leave your receiver on, it can stay in constant communication with GPS satellites to see how your location is changing.

Defense Satellite Communication System (DSCS)

Applications for military satellites may include relaying encrypted communication, nuclear monitoring, observing enemy movements, early warning of missile launches, eavesdropping on terrestrial radio links, radar imaging and photography (using what are essentially large telescopes that take pictures of militarily interesting areas).

Communications satellites are often used for military communications applications, such as Global Command and Control Systems. Examples of military systems that use communication satellites are the MILSTAR (Military Strategic and Tactical Relay), the DSCS, and the FLT-SATCOM (Fleet Satellite Communications System) of the United States, NATO (The North Atlantic Treaty Organization) satellites, United Kingdom satellites (eg. Skynet), and satellites of the former Soviet Union.

DSCS is a military satellite constellation placed in geosynchronous orbit to provide high-volume, secure voice and data communications. The Defense Satellite Communications System (DSCS) provides the United States with military communications to support globally distributed military users.

The first DSCS II launch was in 1971. DSCS went through three major phases - IDCSP (Interim Defense Communication Satellite Program), DSCS-II, and DSCS-III. Since the first launch, DSCS has been the "workhorse" of military satellite communications. All DSCS III satellites have exceeded their 10-year design life.

DSCS II provided secure voice and data communications for the U.S. military. The program was managed by the Defense Communications Agency (DCA), now the Defense Information Systems Agency.

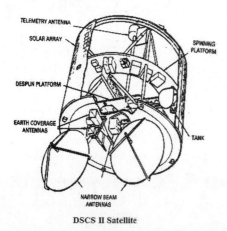

DSCS II Satellite

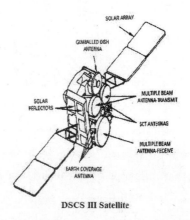

DSCS III Satellite

DSCS III, the most recent configuration, provides uninterrupted secure voice and high data rate communications to DOD users, essential tools in monitoring events and deploying and sustaining forces anywhere in the world.

Air Force Space Command operates ten Phase III DSCS satellites that orbit the earth at an altitude of more than 22,000 miles. Each satellite uses six super high frequency transponder channels capable of providing secure voice and high rate data communications. DSCS III also carries a single-channel transponder for disseminating emergency action and force direction messages to nuclear-capable forces.

The space vehicles were spin stabilized with a de-spun antenna platform. The body was mounted with solar cells which produced 535 watts. Three NiCd batteries provided electrical power and it was supported by a hydrazine propulsion subsystem.

According to the USAF, in early 2008 most of the satellites were still working. DSCS operations are currently run by the 3d Space Operations Squadron out of Schriever AFB.

The DSCS system has been an extremely valuable asset for supporting military and government communications over the past several decades.

Cyberspace and Cyber Warfare

In current usage the term "cyberspace" stands for the global network of interdependent information technology infrastructures, telecommunications networks and computer processing systems. As a social experience, individuals can interact, exchange ideas, share information, provide social support, conduct business, direct actions, create artistic media, play games, engage in political discussion, and so on, using this global network.

Cyber warfare refers to politically motivated hacking to conduct sabotage and espionage. Government security expert Richard A. Clarke, in his book Cyber War (May 2010), defines "cyber warfare" as "actions by a nation-state to penetrate another nation's computers or networks for the purposes of causing damage or disruption". The Economist describes cyber warfare as "the fifth domain of warfare", and William J. Lynn, U.S. Deputy Secretary of Defense, states that "as a doctrinal matter, the Pentagon has formally recognized cyberspace as a new domain in warfare . . . [which] has become just as critical to military operations as land, sea, air, and space".

In recent years, cyber warfare has become an issue of much concern among the major nations on the planet, and virtually every national military now has a branch dedicated to both conducting and defending against cyber warfare.

As the world becomes more networked, more crucial systems become susceptible to attacks in cyberspace. Although certain military systems remain accessible only by being present at a terminal on site, the vast majority of critical systems that control modern nations are now tied into the Internet in some way or another. While these systems are defended by high levels of security, they are nonetheless breakable, and cyber warfare concerns itself with finding weaknesses and exploiting them.

Examples of cyber warfare:

· In 1998, the United States hacked into Serbia's air defense system to compromise air traffic control and facilitate the bombing of Serbian targets.

· In 2007, in Estonia, a botnet of over a million computers brought down government, business and media websites across the country. The attack was suspected to have originated in Russia, motivated by political tension between the two countries.

· Also in 2007, an unknown foreign party hacked into high tech and military agencies in the United States and downloaded terabytes of information.

The most effective protection against cyber warfare attacks is securing information and networks. Security updates should be applied to all systems — including those that are not considered critical — because any vulnerable system can be co-opted and used to carry out attacks. Measures to mitigate the potential damage of an attack include comprehensive disaster recovery planning that includes provisions for extended outages.

Task 2 Answer the following questions.

1. Who originates GPS and what is it for?

2. What should a GPS receiver know in order to make the calculation?

3. What is the general function of DSCS?

4. What is cyber warfare?

5. What can we do to avoid being attacked on cyberspace and secure information?

Task 3 Complete the following translation tasks.

1. Chinese into English

1）全球定位系统体型庞大、造价昂贵，涉及很多独创技术，但其工作原理却非常简单、直观。

2）GPS 接收机通过分析从 GPS 卫星上得到的高频率、低功率无线信号而得出这些结果。

3）标准的 GPS 接收机不仅能确定你在地图上的特定位置，而且能够在地图上跟踪你的移动路径。

4）自第一次发射后，DSCS 已经成为军事卫星通信的"主力"。所有 DSCS III 卫星均已超过其十年的设计寿命。

5）作为一种社交体验，个人可以使用这个全球网络进行互动、交流思想、共享信息、提供社会支援、开展业务、指引行动、创建艺术媒体、玩游戏、参与政治讨论等。

2. English into Chinese

The most effective protection against cyber warfare attacks is securing information and networks. Security updates should be applied to all systems — including those that are not considered critical — because any vulnerable system can be co-opted and used to carry out attacks. Measures to mitigate the potential damage of an attack include comprehensive disaster recovery planning that includes provisions for extended outages.

Task 4 Give an oral presentation in class on the following topics.

1. A Brief Description of the GPS

2. Cyberspace and Cyber Warfare

Part II Watching to Speak

Topic 1 GPS

Task 1 Why is GPS originally developed?

Task 2 What is necessary to find a person's location?

Task 3 Tick the areas that GPS can be applied into according to the video.

Task 4 Put the following sentences into the right order. Give a presentation on how GPS determines a person's location.
   a) give your altitude, speed and direction
   b) find out the four satellites directly above you
   c) turn on the GPS receiver
   d) determine the range
   e) find where the GPS receiver is
   f) broadcast signals
   g) do mathematics using the known location of satellites and range
   Correct order:_____

Task 5 Which of the following cannot be determined by a GPS?
   A. when you may arrive at your destination
   B. how you are changing your route
   C. how long you've been traveling
   D. how fast you are traveling

Task 6 Oral presentation: If you want to trace the enemy as they move, what can you do by using a GPS?

Topic 2 DSCS

Task 1 What is the Air Force responsible for?

Task 2 Identify the four satellites' locations on the map according to the video.

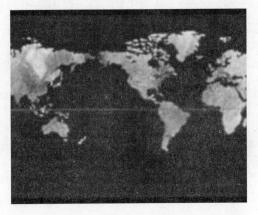

Task 3 Which of the following statements is not true?

A. The communication satellites are in sequence orbit, so from the ground they appear to be stationary.

B. The communication equipment handles 1,300 voice channels.

C. They each has a 10,000 diameter view covers the whole earth area.

D. Two spare satellites are available on-orbit to provide rapid replacement of failed satellites.

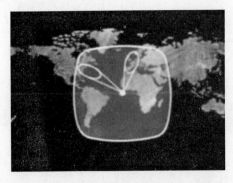
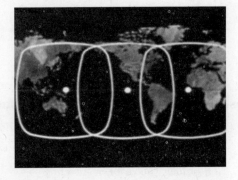

Task 4 Fill in the form information about the two beam antennas.

antenna	area covered (in diameter)	location

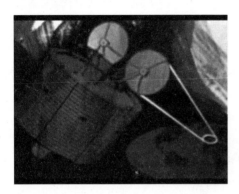

Task 5 When and why were the two new advanced developed DSCS IIIs launched?

Task 6 What can be expected from the launch of DSCS III?

Task 7 Oral presentation: Talk with your partner about DSCS. You may refer to the following words and sentence patterns.

orbit   checkout   in-orbit   stationary   launch   deliver

The Air Force is responsible for the DSCS program. DSCS consists of four active satellites, one over the eastern Atlantic, one over ... , a third is located over ... , and there is a fourth over ... information is received and transmitted by... DSCS III satellites will be delivered to fulfill ... needs and to meet ... conditions, serving our nation's defense needs.

Topic 3 Cyberspace and Cyber Warfare

Task 1 Fill in the blanks with missing words.

Because of the wide use of cyber space and our dependence on it, we have an inherent (1)_____ . That is why it is vital we defend it (2)_____ . Generally in warfare, you have an (3)_____ enemy, a force that is (4)_____ by a country, has a nation's (5)_____ . The cyberspace attacks can occur on an (6)_____ basis, anybody with a $200 laptop and the right skill sets, can go in cyberspace.

Task 2　Choose the right answer for the following questions.

1. Which of the following is not the reason why cyberspace has become a potential danger?

A) There is a wide use of cyberspace.

B) Cyberspace is not safe itself.

C) Individuals have easy access to the cyberspace.

D) People become very dependent on the internet.

2. Which one of the following examples is not mentioned to show that cyberspace is widely used?

A) Power system is controlled by computer system.

B) Water supply is managed by computer system.

C) Nuclear weapon is regulated by computer system.

D) Weapons can be purchased through the computer.

3. Which is the best topic for this video clip?

A) Cyberspace – Blessing or Curse?

B) Cyberspace – the Future Premier Battlefield

C) Cyberspace and Modern War

D) The Multi-function of Cyberspace

Task 3　Why does the Captain regard cyberspace as the future battlefield?

Task 4　Try to imagine the warfare in 2050, how could computer technology influence the battlefield. Report your vision as a commander of the future warfare to the class.

Part III　Scenario Simulation

Work in pairs and small groups. Act out the following scenarios with the language you have learned in this unit.

Scenario 1　TV interviews

Instructions: One of you acts as the interviewer and the other as the engineer. Talk about the function and application of GPS and how it works.

Scenario 2　Class Debate on the Cyber Warfare

Instructions: The class will be divided into two groups to debate on the benefits and potential dangers of cyberspace in military use. Organize your thoughts, write down the major points on the blackboard and briefly explain each point.

New Words

1. espionage 间谍活动
2. ingenuity 独创性；精巧
3. simultaneous 同时发生的；同步的
4. encrypt 加密的，设密码的
5. eavesdrop 偷听，窃听
6. premier 第一的；最初的
7. hack 非法访问计算机系统和数据库的活动
8. mitigate 减轻；缓和
9. sabotage 破坏
10. botnet 僵尸网络（被某程序感染的计算机网络,该程序接收程序创建者指令,向互联网大量主机发送不请自来的邮件、攻击网络等）
11. terabyte 1000 吉（千兆）字节（GB）；兆兆位（量度信息单位）
12. rotation （卫星）旋转；循环
13. trilateration ［测］三边测量（术）
14. geosynchronous 与地球的相对位置不变的, geosynchronous satellite 同步轨道卫星
15. transponder 异频雷达收发机
16. NiCd batteries 镍镉电池（一种流行的蓄电池）
17. hydrazine propulsion （卫星）单元肼推进系统

Military Terms

1. DOD (Department of Defense) 美国国防部
2. DCA (the Defense Communications Agency) 美国国防通信署（旧名称），现改为：the Defense Information Systems Agency 美国国防信息系统局

Cultural Notes

1. Military Strategic and Tactical (MILSTAR) "军事星"系统（军事战略与战术中继卫星）

Originally meaning Military Strategic and Tactical Relay, is a constellation of communications satellites in geostationary orbit, which are operated by the United States Air Force, and provide secure and jam resistant worldwide communications to meet the requirements of the Armed Forces of the United States.

2. Fleet Satellite Communications System (FLTSATCOM also FLTSAT) 美国舰队

卫星通信系统

Fleet Satellite Communications System was a satellite communication system of the U.S. Navy which was used for UHF radio communications between ships, submarines, airplanes and ground stations of the Navy.

3. Schriever Air Force Base (Schriever AFB) 施里弗空军基地

A base of the United States Air Force located approximately 10 miles (16 kilometers) east of Peterson AFB near Colorado Springs in El Paso Country, United States.

Unit 7 Missile Defense

> **Synopsis**
>
> Do you want to know some missiles and the categories of them? Unit 7, *Missile Defense*, provides you the brief introduction of some missiles and how they detect and target at their objectives. It illustrates the targeting, guidance and flying systems for you to have a general understanding of missile defense.

Learning Objectives

1. to know about the basic knowledge of categories of missiles
2. to learn to describe missiles with idiomatic expressions
3. to understand the significance of missiles in detecting at their targets

Part I Reading to Know

Task 1 Read the text.

Missile Defense

Missile defense is a system, weapon, or technology involved in the detection, tracking, interception, and destruction of attacking missiles. Originally conceived as a defense against clear-armed Intercontinental Ballistic Missiles (ICBMs), its application has broadened to include shorter-ranged non-nuclear tactical and theater missiles.

Guided Missile

In a modern military usage, a missile, or guided missile, is a self-propelled guided weapon system, as opposed to an unguided self-propelled munition, referred to as just a rocket. Missiles have four system components: targeting and/or guidance, flight system, engine, and warhead. Missiles come in types adapted for different purposes: surface-to-surface and air-to-surface missiles (ballistic, cruise, anti-ship, anti-tank, etc.), surface-to-air missiles (anti-aircraft and anti-ballistic), air-to-air missiles, and anti-satellite missiles. All known existing missiles are designed to be propelled during powered flight by chemical reactions inside a rocket engine, jet engine, or other type of engine. Non-self-propelled airborne explosive devices are generally referred to as shells and usually have a shorter range than missiles.

Guidance Systems

Missiles may be targeted in a number of ways. The most common method is to use some form of radiation, such as infrared, lasers or radio waves, to guide the missile onto its target. This radiation may emanate from the target (such as the heat of an engine or the radio waves from an enemy radar), it may be provided by the missile itself (such as a radar) or it may be provided by a friendly third party (such as the radar of the launch vehicle/platform, or a laser designator operated by friendly infantry). The first two are often known as fire-and-forget as they need no further support or control from the launch vehicle/platform in order to function. Another method is to use a TV camera—using either visible light or infrared—in order to see the target. The picture may be used either by a human operator who steers the missile onto its target, or by a computer doing much the same job. One of the more bizarre guidance methods instead used a pigeon to steer the missile to its target. Many missiles use a combination of two or more of the above methods, to improve accuracy and the chances of a successful engagement.

A guided missile is an unmanned explosive-carrying vehicle that moves above the earth's surface in a flight path controlled by an external or internal source. There are many kinds of guided missiles, but all have the same ultimate function: destroy enemy "targets", i. e., personnel, tanks, vehicles, airplanes, ships, and weapons, including attacking missiles.

Some missiles attack targets at long distances — thousands of miles — like the ICBM (Intercontinental Ballistic Missile). These are "strategic" missiles.

Other missiles are used offensively or defensively over shorter distances — from a few to a few hundred miles. These are "tactical" missiles.

Targeting Systems

Another method is to target the missile by knowing the location of the target, and using a guidance system such as INS, TERCOM or GPS. This guidance system guides the missile by knowing the missile's current position and the position of the target, and then calculating a course between them. This job can also be performed somewhat crudely by a human operator who can see the target and the missile, and guides it using either cable or radio based remote-control, or by an automatic system that can simultaneously track the target and the missile. Furthermore, some missiles use initial targeting, sending them to a target area, where they will switch to primary targeting, using either radar or IR targeting to acquire the target.

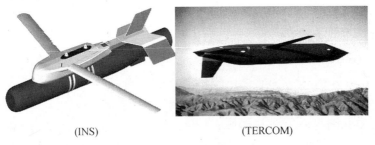

(INS)   (TERCOM)

Flight System

Whether a guided missile uses a targeting system, a guidance system or both, it needs a flight system. The flight system uses the data from the targeting or guidance system to maneuver the missile in flight, allowing it to counter inaccuracies in the missile or to follow a moving target. There are two main systems: vectored thrust (for missiles that are powered throughout the guidance phase of their flight) and aerodynamic maneuvering.

Engine

Missiles are powered by an engine, generally either a type of rocket or jet engine. Rockets are generally of the solid fuel type for ease of maintenance and fast deployment, although some larger ballistic missiles use liquid fuel rockets. Jet engines are generally used in cruise missiles, most commonly of the turbojet type, due to its relative simplicity and low frontal area. Turbofans and ramjets are the only other common forms of jet engine propulsion, although any type of engine could theoretically be used. Missiles often have multiple engine stages, particularly in those launched from the surface. These stages may all be of similar types or may include a mix of engine types — for example, surface-launched cruise missiles often have a rocket booster for launching and a jet engine for sustained flight.

(Russian turbofan)

Warhead

Missiles generally have one or more explosive warheads, although other weapon types may also be used. The warhead or warheads of a missile provides its primary destructive power (many missiles have extensive secondary destructive power due to the high kinetic energy of the weapon and unburnt fuel that may be on board). Warheads are most commonly of the high explosive type, often employing shaped charges to exploit the accuracy of a guided weapon to destroy hardened targets. Other warhead types include sub munitions, incendiaries, nuclear weapons, chemical, biological or radiological weapons or kinetic energy penetrators. Warheadless missiles are often used for testing and training purposes.

Categories

Missiles are generally categorized by their launch platform and intended target. According to different launch platforms, there are Surface-to-surface missile (SSM), Air-to-air missile (AAM), Air-to-surface missile (ASM), Surface-to-air missile (SAM), Ballistic missile and Intercontinental ballistic missile (ICBM), etc. For the intended targets, there are Anti-ballistic missile (ABM), Anti-ship missile (AShM), Anti-submarine missile, Anti-tank missile (ATGM), Anti-satellite weapon (ASAT) and so on. By different guidance, there are Anti-radiation, Wire guidance, Infrared guidance, Beam riding, Laser guidance, Active radar guidance, Semi-active radar guidance, Unguided rockets.

In broadest terms, these will either be surface (ground or water) or air, and then sub-categorized by range and the exact target type (such as anti-tank or anti-ship). Many weapons are designed to be launched from both surface or the air, and a few are designed to attack either surface or air targets (such as the ADATS missile). Most weapons require some modification in order to be launched from the air or surface, such as adding boosters to the surface-launched version.

Surface-to-Surface

A surface-to-surface missile (SSM) or ground-to-ground missile (GGM) is a missile designed to be launched from the ground or the sea and strike targets on land or at sea. They may be fired from hand-held or vehicle mounted devices, from fixed installations, or from a ship. They are often powered by a rocket motor or sometimes fired by an explosive charge, since the launching platform is typically stationary or moving slowly. They usually have fins and/or wings for lift and stability, although hyper-velocity or short-ranged missiles may utilize body lift or fly a ballistic trajectory. The V-1 flying bomb was the first operational surface-to-surface missile. Contemporary surface-to-surface missiles are usually guided.

(Maverick)

Air-to-air

An air-to-air missile (AAM) is a missile fired from an aircraft for the purpose of destroying another aircraft. AAMs are typically powered by one or more rocket motors, usually solid fuelled but sometimes liquid fuelled. Ramjet engines, as used on the MBDA Meteor (currently in development), are emerging as propulsion that will enable future medium-range missiles to maintain higher average speed across their engagement envelope.

Air-to-air missiles are broadly put in two groups. Those designed to engage opposing aircraft at ranges of less than 30 km are known as short-range or "within visual range" missiles (SRAAMs or WVRAAMs) and are sometimes called "dogfight" missiles because they are designed to optimize their agility rather than range. Most use infrared guidance and are called heat-seeking missiles. In contrast, medium- or long-range missiles (MRAAMs or LRAAMs), which both fall under the category of beyond visual range missiles (BVRAAMs), tend to rely upon radar guidance, of which there are many forms. Some modern ones use inertial guidance and/or "mid-course updates" to get the missile close enough to use an active homing sensor. The US Navy and US Air Force began equipping guided missiles in 1956, deploying the USAF's AIM-4 Falcon and the USN's AIM-7 Sparrow and AIM-9 Sidewinder.

(AIM-9 Sidewinder)

Air-to-Surface

An air-to-surface missile (ASM) or air-to-ground missile (AGM or ATGM) is a missile designed to be launched from military aircraft (bombers, attack aircraft, fighter aircraft or other kinds) and strike ground targets on land, at sea, or both. They are similar to guided glide bombs but to be deemed a missile, they usually contain some kind of propulsion system. The two most common propulsion systems for air-to-surface missiles are rocket motors and jet engines. Guidance for air-to-surface missiles is typically via laser guidance, infrared guidance, optical guidance or via GPS signals. The type of guidance depends on the type of target. Ships, for example, may be detected via passive or active radar, while this would not work very well against land targets which typically do not contain such a large mass of metal surrounded by empty space.

The AGM-65 Maverick is an air-to-surface tactical missile (AGM) designed for close air support. The most widely produced precision-guided missile in the Western world, it is effective against a wide range of tactical targets, including armor, air defenses, ships, ground transportation and fuel storage facilities. Originally designed and built by Hughes Missile Systems, development of the AGM-65 spanned from 1966 to 1972, after which it entered service with the United States Air Force in August 1972. Since then, it has been exported to more than 30 countries and is certified on 25 aircraft. The AGM-88 High-speed Anti-Radiation Missile (HARM) is a tactical, air-to-surface missile. It is designed to home in on electronic transmissions coming from surface-to-air radar systems. It was originally developed as a replacement for the AGM-45 Shrike and AGM-78 Standard ARM system.

Intercontinental Ballistic Missile (ICBM)

An Intercontinental Ballistic Missile (ICBM) is a ballistic missile with a minimum range of more than 5,500 kilometers (3,400 mi) primarily designed for nuclear weapons delivery (delivering one or more nuclear warheads). Similarly conventional, chemical and biological weapons can also be delivered with varying effectiveness. Most modern designs support multiple independently targetable reentry vehicles (MIRVs), allowing a single missile to carry several warheads, each of which can strike a different target.

Early ICBMs had limited accuracy that allowed them to be used only against the largest targets such as cities. They were seen as a "safe" basing option, one that would keep the deterrent force close to home where it would be difficult to attack. Attacks against military targets, if desired, still demanded the use of a manned bomber. Second and third generation designs dramatically improved accuracy to the point where even the smallest point targets can be successfully attacked. The Minuteman (LGM-30G Minuteman III) is a strategic weapon system using a ballistic missile of intercontinental range.

 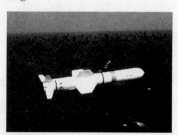

(LGM-30G Minuteman)

ICBMs are differentiated by having greater range and speed than other ballistic missiles: intermediate-range ballistic missiles (IRBMs), medium-range ballistic missiles (MRBMs), short-range ballistic missiles (SRBMs)—these shorter range ballistic missiles are known collectively as theatre ballistic missiles. There is no single, standardized definition of what ranges would be categorized as intercontinental, intermediate, medium, or short.

Task 2 Answer the following questions.

1. How many system components do missiles have?

2. What are the common methods used to guide missiles onto their targets?

3. What's the difference between strategic missiles and tactical missiles?

4. How can guidance system help missile to know the location of the target?

5. What are the two main flying systems?

6. What is Intercontinental Ballistic Missile and what is it designed for?

Task 3 Complete the following translation tasks.

1. Chinese to English

1）尽管从理论上讲可以使用任何类型的引擎,但是涡扇发动机和冲压式喷气发动机是常见的动力推进喷气发动机。

2）大多数现代导弹设计支持分导多弹头导弹,允许一个导弹携带多个弹头,每一个弹头可以打击不同的目标。

3）AGM65C型"小牛"空对地导弹是特意为对抗指定激光目标设计的,它担任着近距离空中支援角色。

4）针对地面防空雷达,20世纪60年代研制成功了反辐射导弹,美国先后装备了AGM-45"百舌鸟"、AGM-78"标准"和AGM-88"哈姆"三代反辐射导弹。

5）对抗军事目标,如果需要的话,仍可以使用有人轰炸机。

2. English into Chinese

Whether a guided missile uses a targeting system, a guidance system or both, it needs a flight system. The flight system uses the data from the targeting or guidance system to maneuver the missile in flight, allowing it to counter inaccuracies in the missile or to follow a moving target. There are two main systems: vectored thrust (for missiles that are powered throughout the guidance phase of their flight) and aerodynamic maneuvering.

Task 4　Give an oral presentation in class on the following topics.

1. Give a brief introduction to four main component systems of missiles.

2. Summarize the categories of missiles and describe the one that you are familiar with.

Part II　Watching to Speak

Topic 1　AIM-9 Sidewinder

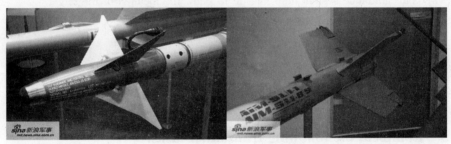

Task 1　Watch the video clip and tell your desk-mate what it is about.

Task 2　Watch, write down the crew members in the missile.

Task 3　Watch again and write down the work done by each member.

Crew member	Work

Task 4　Watch again and put the following sentences in order.

a) Command and control press the button.

b) The helmsman returns to the seat and adjusts the trajectory of the missile.

c) The lookout locates the target.

d) The blaster detonates the missile.

e) The pitcher starts throwing the ball.

f) They abandon the missile.

g) The missile is flying unguided.

h) The missile reaches its maximum speed.

Correct order: _____

Task 5 Watch the video and answer the questions.

1. What is the main feature of AIM-9L?

2. How many AIM-9P Sidewinder missiles are developed and introduced?

3. Who will employ the AIM-9P Sidewinder missiles?

Task 6 Watch the video again and fill in the blanks.

The improved AIM-9P has recently completed an (1) _____ Air Force test establishing the level of (2) _____ improvements to the sidewinder (3) _____ missile system. Hawd Aerospace has completed missile production experience including (4) _____, (5) _____ and (6) _____ of more than (7) _____ all-up-round (8) _____ missiles.

Task 7 Talk with your partner about the components of the missiles.

The missile consists of ... First, ... Second, ...

Topic 2 AGM-65 Maverick

81

Task 1　Watch the video clip and tell your desk-mate what you know about Maverick.

Task 2　Watch the video again and fill in the blanks.

Maverick Family	Primary Function	Launch Weight	Guidance System	Warhead
				/
				/

Task 3　Watch the video clip and complete the following sentences.

　　1. The AGM-65 Maverick is the Air Force's versatile (1)＿＿＿＿ propelled (2) ＿＿＿＿ missile.

　　2. The Maverick was designed to attack targets such as (3)＿＿＿＿, parked aircraft, armored personnel carriers, (4)＿＿＿＿, radar or missile sites and (5)＿＿＿＿.

Task 4　Watch the video and answer the questions.

　　1. How many Maverick missiles can be loaded on an aircraft?

　　2. What is the Maverick developed primarily for?

　　3. Why is the survival ability of the flight crews increased by employing Maverick?

　　4. What kind of warhead does Maverick have?

Task 5　Watch the video again and tick True (T) or False (F) about the following statements.

　　1. The several different targets can be attacked on a single mission.　☐ T ☐ F
　　2. The AGM-65E is guided by radar.　☐ T ☐ F
　　3. The weight of the warhead of AGM-65E is 130 pounds.　☐ T ☐ F
　　4. The fuse of Maverick is fixed.　☐ T ☐ F
　　5. Among the Maverick family, various Mavericks have nothing in common.　☐ T ☐ F

Task 6 Talk with your partner about your knowledge about AGM-65 Maverick. You may refer to the following sentence pattern.

Maverick is a precision guided ... missile in the ... class. The Maverick missile family consists of several types of missiles used for different applications. The unique Maverick includes AGM-65A which is ...

Topic 3   JAGM (Joint Air-to-Ground Missile)

Task 1 Watch the video clip and discuss in your group what it is about.

Task 2 Watch again and note down the three characteristics of the missile.
 1. _____
 2. _____
 3. _____

Task 3 Watch the video and tick True (T) or False (F) about the following statements.
 1. JAGM is a 90-million- dollar research development investment. ☐ T ☐ F
 2. The Tri-Mode Seeker is designed for all-weather detecting. ☐ T ☐ F
 3. The next generation design aims at moving and static targets. ☐ T ☐ F
 4. The Multi-Effect Warhead is not lethal against soft targets. ☐ T ☐ F
 5. The Advanced Propulsion can double the ranges over Hellfire. ☐ T ☐ F

Task 4 Watch the video clip and match the items that agree to each other.

  mobile layer defense   Apache Longbow Block III
  advanced aircraft   make it safe
  select targets of interests   JAGM

a 900-million-dollar investment   on and off board sensors

Task 5 Watch the video clip and fill in the blanks with what you hear.

JAGM provides the (1) _____ laser to the challenges of asymmetric warfare, design (2) _____ to meet the demands of UN leader. It (3) _____ their capabilities to identify targets of the interests. It allows for the engagement of the target of the opportunities in the way not possible with the (4) _____. The (5) _____ of infrared JAGM meet a wide range of demands and put it low in damage and effectiveness against the diverse targets. JAGM, a smart investment, a (6) _____ to address the four spectrum of (7) _____ providing complying cooperation advantages and life-cycle (8) _____ for the future.

Task 6 Watch the whole video clip and share the main characteristics, functions and capabilities of the missile with your partner.

Part III Scenario Simulation

Work in groups. Act out the following scenarios with the language you have learned in this unit.

Scenario 1 Advertisement for a missile

Instructions: Advertise for a missile you like. Don't forget to tell the features of the missile, including its warhead, guidance system, attacking objects and so on. Design your advertisement and make it attractive.

Scenario 2 Missiles parade

Instructions: You may fall into 2 groups, one group stands for China, the other stands for the US. Compare the missiles of the same category and discuss their weaknesses and strengths. You may compare the missiles in the following aspects: propulsion, range, warhead, speed, guidance system, cost and performance.

New Words

1. theater missiles 战区导弹
2. interception 截取;拦截
3. self-propelled munition 自航弹药

4. infrared 红外;红外线的
5. emanate from 发源于;出自
6. infantry 步兵
7. fire-and-forget 发后自寻的,发射后不管
8. TV camera 电视摄像机
9. INS(Inertial Navigation System)惯性导航系统
10. GPS(Global Position System)全球定位系统
11. vectored thrust 矢量推力
12. aerodynamic maneuvering 气动操纵
13. canard(鸭式飞机的)水平控制和安全面
14. turbojet 涡轮喷气飞机
15. ramjets [航]冲压式喷气发动机
16. trajectory [航][军]弹道

Military Terms
1. TERCOM(terrain contour matching)地形匹配
2. kinetic energy penetrators 动能穿甲弹
3. ADATS(Air Defense Anti-tank System)防空与反坦克系统
4. ICBMs(Intercontinental Ballistic Missiles)洲际弹道导弹

Cultural Notes
1. V-1 flying bomb 德国 V1 飞弹
It is also known as the buzz bomb, or doodlebug—was an early pulse-jet-powered predecessor of the cruise missile. The V-1 was developed at Peenemunde Army Research Centre by the German Luftwaffe during the Second World War.

2. AGM-45 Shrike AGM-45 "百舌鸟"
AGM-45 Shrike is an American anti-radiation missile designed to home in on hostile anti-aircraft radar. The Shrike was developed by the Naval Weapons Center at China Lake in 1963 by mating a seeker head to the rocket body of an AIM-7 Sparrow. It was phased out by U.S. in 1992 and at an unknown time by the Israeli Air Force (the only other major user), and has been superseded by the AGM-88 HARM missile.

3. AGM-78 Standard ARM AGM-78 "标准" 反辐射导弹
Originally developed for the US Navy during the late 1960s, the AGM-78 was created in large part because of the limitations of the AGM-45 Shrike, which suffered from a small warhead, limited range and a poor guidance system. General Dynamics was asked to create an air-launched ARM by modifying the RIM-66 SM-1 surface-to-air missile. This use of an "off the shelf" design greatly reduced development costs, and trials of the new weapon begun in 1967

after only a year of development.

4. MBDA Meteor "流星"空空导弹

Meteor is an active radar guided beyond-visual-range air-to-air missile (BVRAAM) being developed by MBDA. Meteor will offer a multi-shot capability against long range maneuvering targets in a heavy electronic countermeasures (ECM) environment. According to MBDA, Meteor has three to six times the kinematic performance of current air-air missiles of its type.

5. MIRVs 分导多弹头导弹

A multiple independently targetable reentry vehicle (MIRV) is a ballistic missile payload containing several warheads, each capable of being aimed to hit one of a group of targets. By contrast a unitary warhead is a single warhead on a single missile. An intermediate case is the Multiple reentry vehicle (MRV) missile which carries several reentry vehicles which are dispersed but not individually aimed, somewhat like a shotgun.

6. LGM-30G Minuteman III "民兵III"洲际弹道导弹

The LGM-30 Minuteman is a United States land-based intercontinental ballistic missile (ICBM), in service with the United States Air Force Global Strike Command. As of 2014, the LGM-30G Minuteman-III version is the only land-based ICBM in service in the United States. It is one component of the US nuclear triad-the other two parts of the triad being the Trident submarine-launched ballistic missile (SLBM), and nuclear weapons carried by long-range strategic bombers.

7. Fire in the hole 用来警告即将而来的爆炸

It is a warning that an explosive detonation in a confined space is imminent. It originated with miners, who needed to warn their fellows that a charge had been set.

Unit 8   Red Flag Exercise

Synopsis

The Red Flag exercises, held periodically at the Nellis Air Force Base since 1975, are very realistic aerial war games. Do you want to know why it is created and how it is carried out? Unit 8, *Red Flag Exercise*, gives you the exciting and vivid account of different sessions of Red Flag Exercises. It illustrates its procedures, aircraft deployed, missions, briefing and debriefing sessions, etc. in great detail.

Learning Objectives

1. to know about the general procedures of an air combat exercise
2. to learn to talk about air combat war game with idiomatic expressions
3. to understand the significance of air war combat training

Part I   Reading to Know

Task 1   Read the text.

Red Flag Exercises

Red Flag is the most advanced aerial combat training exercise in the world which is hosted by the U.S., originated to train pilots' real air combat capability. Now, the Red Flag exercises, are held periodically at the Nellis Air Force Base. The purpose is to give pilots not only from the U.S., but from NATO and other allied countries an opportunity to practice and refine their skills for real combat situations.

This includes the use of "enemy" hardware and live ammunition for bombing exercises within the Nellis complex. Red Flag is currently the most realistic simulated air-warfare exercise held anywhere in the world.

There are four Red Flags per year, and each Red Flag has one to three 2-week periods with different players. So, each Red Flag is 2 to 6 weeks in total.

History

The origin of Red Flag was the unacceptable performance of U.S. Air Force fighter pilots and weapon systems officers (WSO) in air combat maneuvering (ACM) (air-to-air combat) during the Vietnam War. Although the United States air force achieved a roughly 10-to-1 kill ratio over communist forces during the Korean War, by the time of the Vietnam War the ratio had fallen to about 2-to-1, and for a period during 1972 it fell to 1-to-1.

Among the several factors resulting in the poor performance was a lack of realistic ACM training. At that time, nearly all USAF fighter pilots and WSO were unpracticed in maneuvering against dissimilar aircraft because of a concurrent Air Force emphasis on flying safety.

An Air Force analysis showed that a pilot's chances of survival in combat dramatically increased after he had completed 10 combat missions. As a result, Red Flag was created in 1975 to offer USAF pilots and weapon systems officers the opportunity to fly 10 realistically simulated combat missions in a safe training environment with measurable results.

Operations

Red Flag is administered by the Tactical Fighter Weapons Center at Nellis. There are usually two or three sorties per day (except on weekends): One or two sorties during daytime and one in the evening or at night.

There are two teams, the good guys (Blue Force) and the aggressors (Red Force). The Blue Team is composed of the various guest "players" in their native aircraft who are tasked with defending and attacking. The Red Team is composed of Nellis AFB-based very experienced pilots specially trained for this purpose, flying F-16 aircraft with special camouflage to mimic Russian and Ex-Warsaw Pact Country Camouflage.

Before each Flag mission, special orientation flights are set up by Nellis so that unfamiliar pilots can get an overflight of the ranges, names of places, altitudes, etc. These are usually done in C-130 Hercules and UH-60 Black Hawks.

During a typical day of Red Flag, each Blue Force sends up approximately two to four packages, each containing up to 20 to 30 aircraft. Each battle lasts for 2 to 3 hours.

Scenarios are shaped to meet each exercise's specific training objectives. In one typical scenario, the Red Forces start the day over in the west side of the ranges, while the Blue Force starts out from the east. The objective for the Blue Team is to destroy targets in Ranges 74 thru 76. The Red Team, of course, tries their best to keep them from getting there. Both teams usually meet in the airspace where they engage in very realistic dogfights.

In each Red Flag period, besides the air combat training, a few days are set aside for special operations such as combat search and rescue, airdrops and transport exercises using the C-130, C-160 and many Helicopters.

After the air combat, a key element of the Red Flag Game follows. It is "debriefing", which is partially enabled by a special pod.

All aircraft involved in the exercises are equipped with this special pod which is located on one of the hard points. The pod is called an "AIS" or Airborne Instrumentation Subsystem. This is linked to the aircraft's on-board electrical, avionics and weapons systems. This pod then communicates directly with special systems located in ground stations. These are called the Tracking and Communications Subsystem (TCS). From here the feed is transmitted via microwaves to the Computer and Computed Subsystem (CCS) based at Nellis. All information gathered comes up on large screens and the personnel are then able to "see" what the pilots are seeing, where the bombs drop, what the situation is in the "air-war" and so on.

All pilots and crew involved are then, after landing, debriefed via the DDS (Display and Debrief Subsystem) to view their actions, wins, mistakes and so on.

Ranges

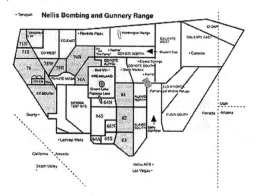

The actual area reserved for military flying in Red Flag is over 10,000,000 acres. The Range has over fifty different types of targets which include Trains, Armored Vehicles, Industrial complexes, High threat targets such as Radars, SAMs and AAA placements, convoys, railways and bridges and also complete airfields. Some convoys are believed to be over 17 miles long incorporating every type of vehicle NATO would come up against. Complete Railways of over 10 miles long with complete trains are placed on the northern ranges and also the industrial complexes are very large multi-building areas. All high threat simulators such as the radars are soviet made and operate on the exact frequency they would in time of war detecting inbound aircraft at ranges over 250 miles relaying target information to the manned stations ... it is all extremely realistic.

Red Flag is held over the whole Nellis Gunnery and bombing Range Complex and also in the large Military Operating Areas (MOA).

The Nellis Range and MOA's are split up into sub-sections which are the following:

Tonopah Electronic Combat Range (TECR). This is the main electronic combat range with manned high threat simulators.

Tolicha Peak (TPECR), which incorporates a mock "Korean" designed airfield with many mothballed aircraft located there as targets.

Range 61, 62 and 64, used for bombing and gunnery training and also used for simulated nuclear bomb delivery training.

Range 71, 74, 75 and 76 are all used for Live and Dumb Bombing and gunnery training on high value high threat targets.

Dart East, Dart West and Dart South are used for live and practice air-air engagements with guns and missiles.

All of the above sectors are used for air-air training and are all used for Subsonic and Supersonic interceptions and dogfights. Flight Levels used around the Desert MOA in the sectors mentioned above range from 100ft Above Ground Level (AGL) to 50,000ft AGL. These sectors are extremely busy during Red Flag. Sonic Booms can be heard throughout the day in these areas.

Participants

Participants on Blue force have been extremely varied and a lot are not even NATO members but are allies to NATO and the USA. These include over the years since the 70s: The United Kingdom which is a major player in All Flag and Air Warrior Exercises using Tornado GR-1 and F-3, Jaguar, Harrier, VC-10 Tankers, C-130 (special forces), AWACS and TriStars (tankers) and have come home with many Bombing and ECM trophies; Venezuela using F-16s; Netherlands using F-16s; Norway using F-16s; Australia using F-111s; Denmark using F16s; Korea using F16s; Egypt using various types; Germany using F-4s and Mig29s; France using Mirage 2000s; Singapore with F16s; Belgium with F16s; Greece with Mirage 2000s and F-4s; Italy with F-104s; Jordan with F16s; Turkey with F16s; Saudi Arabia using F15s; Spain using F/A-18s; not to mention USAF, USN and USMC using near enough every front line aircraft in US inventory.

Task 2 Answer the following questions.

1. How many Red Flags are held each year? And how long does each last?

2. What is the origin of Red Flag Exercise?

3. What are the two teams in Red Flag?

4. What is the typical scenario given by the text?

5. What is the function of the pod called AIS?

6. Can you give some examples of high value high threat targets in Red Flag?

Task 3   Complete the following translation tasks.

1. Chinese into English

1）红旗军演是目前世界上最接近实战的空战演习。

2）美国空军在朝鲜战争中的战损是10:1,而在越南战争中却降到了2:1。

3）在每一次红旗军演开始前,内利斯空军基地都安排了特殊的适应飞行。外国飞行员们乘坐"大力神"运输机和"黑鹰"直升机鸟瞰整个靶场,熟悉地名、地理高度等。

4）每一次演习的具体训练目标将决定演习中的各个想定。

5）蓝军在空中接敌,与红军进行近乎实战的空中格斗。

2. English into Chinese

  All high threat simulators, such as the Radars, are Soviet made and operate on the exact frequency they would in time of war detecting inbound aircraft at ranges over 250 miles relaying target information to the manned stations.

Task 4   Give an oral presentation in class on the following topics.

1. Brief Description of the Ranges for Red Flag

2. Introduction to Red Flag

Part II   Watching to Speak

Topic 1   General Introduction

Task 1   Watch the video clip and fill in the blanks.

  United States Air Force pilots are a (1)_____. They represent (2)_____ in a deadly plane field. As the world becomes ever more dangerous, their actions and those of their (3)_____ and (4)_____ become more and more crucial to success in combat. Less than 6 miles from Las Vegas strip, extraordinary (5)_____ take place. Pilots and crews train in the world's most (6)_____ war game arena ever devised. It's called Red Flag. And depicts the best of the best in (7)_____. Designed to (8)_____ actual warfare on an unprecedented (9)_____.

Task 2 Watch, tick and fill in the form with related information.

Red Flag

Home of Red Flag	Nellis Air Force Base, Las Vegas, Navada
Purpose	Give the most _____ fighter pilots the lessons they need to _____.
Duration	_____ days
Components	_____ squadrons _____ aircraft _____ maintenance personnel _____ operations personnel
Missions	☐ live ordnance ☐ day missions ☐ living and breathing enemy air force ☐ live ammunition ☐ night missions
Range	rock sand threat

Task 3 Watch the video clip, take notes and talk with your partner about the scenarios.

Real life war scenarios:
Scenario 1. _____
Scenario 2. _____
Scenario 3. _____
Scenario 4. _____
Scenario 5. _____
Scenario 6. _____

Task 4 Watch the video and tick out the aircraft appeared in the Red Flag.

Types of aircraft		
☐ air-to-air fighter	☐ air-to-ground striker	☐ F-117 bomber
☐ KC-135 tanker	☐ C-130 airlift aircraft	☐ J-Star (AWACS)
☐ HH-60 helicopter	☐ B-2 bomber	

Task 5 Watch again and fill in the blanks. You may refer to the following information.

Functions of aircraft		
air-to-air dogfighting	combat search and rescue	bombing
air refueling	electronic surveillance	airlifting
taking out targets on the range		

Type:
Function:

Type:
Function:

Type:
Function:

Type:
Function:

Type:
Function:

Type:
Function:

Type:
Function:

Type:
Function:

Task 6 Work in pairs. Introduce Red Flag Exercise to your partner with the following structure.

Red Flag exercise is the most . . . exercises in the world. It carries out . . . times a year with each session lasting. . . The purpose of the war game is to. . . The general scenarios are. . . In the exercise, you can see every aspect of modern air warfare integrated into the missions. . . . (aircraft and their missions in the Red Flag). Over a hundred aircraft executing . . . makes the Red Flag the most realistic and demanding air war experience in the world.

Topic 2   Air Combat

Task 1   Watch the video clip and answer the following questions.

1. What will the Red Flag participants do before each mission?

2. Who is the founder of the Red Flag and why to create it?

3. What do the participants do in the Suter Hall?

Task 2   Watch the video and tell the scenario to your partner with the map.

Useful expressions	
➤ undergo	• regime change
	• Minister of Defense
➤ threat to use	• scud missile
	• neighboring county
	• biological and chemical weapons
➤ take out	• F-16 Strike Eagles
	• chemical plant

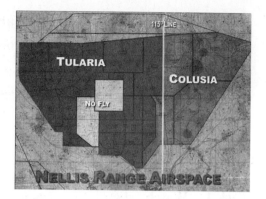

Task 3 Watch the video and answer the following questions.

1. What kind of aircraft does the Blue Force fly?

2. What kind of missile does the aircraft of the Blue Force carry?

3. What is the aim of HARM?

4. What is the capability of Red Aggressors' F-16 armament?

Task 4 Watch the video and fill in the blanks.

A (1) _____ of aircraft move into the airspace arena, (2) _____ aircraft, or AWACS, paints the (3) _____. The electronic order of battle, data is linked to the various aircraft entering the fight. The GCI or (4) _____ controllers, using Soviet methods guide their Red Forces from the ground and determine and dictate what (5) _____ their planes will perform.

Task 5 Watch and tick True (T) or False (F) about the purposes of evaluation and debriefing.

1. To show the Red Flag staff what to be include in the next day mission. ☐ T ☐ F
2. To introduce the next mission to the Blue Force. ☐ T ☐ F
3. To see how the Blue Force is progressing. ☐ T ☐ F
4. To award the good pilots in the Blue Force. ☐ T ☐ F
5. To look at the performance of the Blue Force for themselves. ☐ T ☐ F
6. To draw a conclusion about the training. ☐ T ☐ F
7. To help the Blue Force to know their mistakes and how to fix them. ☐ T ☐ F

Task 6   Talk with your partner about the different sessions of each Red Flag. You may refer to the following sentence patterns.

Before each mission, all the participants will... Based on the training objectives, ... are designed. During the air war combat, the Blue Force... and the Red Force... After each mission, there will be a (an)... which is very important because...

Topic 3   Heading Home

Task 1   Watch, dictate and translate.

On the threat facility wall, there's a quote from Sun Tzu *The Art of War*. "If you (1) _____, (2) _____, you (3) _____. If you (4) _____ (5) _____, for every victory gained you (6) _____. If you (7) _____ (8) _____, you will (9) _____."

Chinese version:

_____

_____

_____

Task 2   Translate the following sentences from *The Art of War*.

1. 攻其不备,出其不意。

_____

2. 能因敌变化而取胜者,谓之神。

_____

3. 善战者,致人而不致于人。

_____

4. 三军可夺气,将军可夺心。

_____

Task 3   Watch the video clip and discuss the influence of Red Flag with your partner.

The 2-week's Red Flag has taught the participants... The sentences "new swords are tested. Old swords have a new edge." shows that ...

Part III   Scenario Simulation

Work in groups. Act out the following scenarios with the language you have learned in this unit.

Scenario 1　Scenario Development

Instructions: work in groups to design the objectives of a training exercise, such as improving the shooting accuracy. Based on the objectives, work out a scenario or several scenarios for the war game. Then one student presented in front of the class. Drawing on the black board while speaking is advised.

Scenario 2　War Game

Instructions: if your group is the Blue Force who are tasked to fly into the heart of the Red Force to protect a C-130 as it lands and drops off troops. Discuss with your groupmates what types of aircraft will you deploy and your reasons. Then present your plan in front of the class.

New words

1. concurrent 同时的
2. complex 综合建筑群
3. mothballed 封存的
4. mimic 模仿
5. camouflage 伪装
6. acre 英亩
7. relay 中继;接力
8. Las Vegas strip 拉斯维加斯大道
9. extraordinary 特别的,非凡的
10. arena 竞技场;舞台
11. depict 描画,描述
12. unprecedented 空前的,无前例的
13. deploy 部署
14. cohesive 有结合力的,有内聚力的

Military Terms

1. aerial war games 空战演习
2. combat 作战
3. live ammunition 实弹
4. air-warfare exercise / aerial combat war game 空战演习
5. sortie 出动架次
6. scenario (演习)想定
7. range 靶场

8. armored 装甲的
9. convoy 护送(车队)
10. radar 雷达
11. inbound 返场的
12. gunnery 重炮;射击
13. aggressor 敌人;入侵者
14. dogfight 空中格斗
15. sonic booms 声震(飞机以超声速飞行时就会产生声震)
16. Airborne Instrumentation Subsystem (AIS) 航空仪表子系统
17. Tracking and Communications Subsystem (TCS) 跟踪与通信子系统
18. DDS (Display and Debrief SubSystem) 显示与任务报告子系统
19. pod 挂舱
20. hardpoint 挂架;挂载点
21. SAM (surface-to-air missile) 地对空导弹
22. AAA (anti-aircraft artillery) 高射炮
23. Above Ground Level (AGL) 离地高度
24. AWACS (Airborne Warning and Control System) 机载报警与控制系统
25. ECM (electronic countermeasure) 电子对抗
26. inventory 武器库
27. Air Expeditionary Force 空军远征军
28. ordnance 军用品
29. high-speed anti-radiation missile (HARM) "哈姆"式导弹(高速反辐射导弹)
30. home in on (靠信号、雷达等)导向目标追踪

Cultural Notes

1. Warsaw Pact 华沙条约

A collective defense treaty among eight communist states of Central and Eastern Europe in existence during the Cold War.

2. Tactical Fighter Weapons Center 美国空军战术战斗机武器中心

3. E-3D Sentry E-3D"哨兵"空中预警机

4. ASRAAM (Advanced Medium-Range Air-to-Air Missile) 高级中程空对空导弹

5. Tornado GR-1 "狂风"多用途战斗机

6. Jaguar "美洲虎"双发超声速战斗机

7. VC-10 Tankers VC-10 空中加油机

8. C-130 "大力神"中型战术运输机,由美国洛克希德·马丁公司(Lockheed Martin)所研发生产

9. *The Art of War* 《孙子兵法》

Unit 9　UN Peacekeeping

> ## Synopsis
>
> Do you know how the UN peacekeepers fulfill operations? What specific tasks are involved in peacekeeping operations? Unit 9, *UN Peacekeeping*, guides you to have a general understanding of the basic knowledge of peacekeeping in simple words. It talks about the history, the common missions and real examples of peacekeeping which finally makes it clear that the peacekeepers are playing an indispensable role in taking measures to deal with threats to the peace of the world.

Learning Objectives

1. to know about the general knowledge of UN peacekeeping operation and forces
2. to learn to talk about peacekeeping tasks with idiomatic expressions
3. to understand the indispensability and arduousness of peacekeeping forces

Part I　Reading to Know

Task 1　Read the text.

On UN Peacekeeping

Traditional peacekeeping had focused mainly on monitoring ceasefire, while today's complex peace operations are very different. Their objective, in essence, is to assist the parties engaged in conflict to pursue their interests through political channels instead.

Peacekeeping is a UN innovation.

The Charter of the United Nations calls upon the peoples of the world "to unite our strength to maintain international peace and security", and charges the Security Council with the task of "determining the existence of any threat to the peace and deciding what measures shall be taken".

Peacekeeping was never mentioned in the Charter as one of the tools to be employed by the United Nations. Yet it took only three years for this whole new technique to be conceived: that of using troops under UN command to keep disputing countries or communities from fighting while peacemaking efforts are pursued. This technique of keeping peace was to be implemented thirteen times in the UN's first forty years. Since then forty new missions have been created, expanding the concept of peacekeeping dramatically and moving into the arena of peacemaking and peace-building.

What is peacekeeping?

Simply speaking, peacekeepers are people helping the parties to a conflict to resolve their differences peacefully. The presence of these people, soldiers, military observers or civilian police, encourage hostile groups not to use arms and instead to keep negotiating for peaceful settlement of disputes.

Most UN peacekeepers—often referred to as "**blue helmets**" because of the blue colour helmets they wear while on duty—have been soldiers, volunteered by their Governments to apply military discipline and training to the task of restoring and maintaining peace: monitoring cease-fires, separating hostile forces and maintaining buffer zones. Civilian police officers, electoral observers, human rights monitors and other civilians have joined UN peacekeepers in recent years. Their tasks range from protecting and delivering humanitarian assistance, to helping former opponents carry out complicated peace agreements. Traditionally, peacekeeping operations fall into two main categories: observer missions and peacekeeping forces. Observer missions usually consist of unarmed military and civilian personnel who monitor the implementation of cease-fire agreements. Peacekeeping forces are composed of lightly armed forces, and include fully equipped infantry contingents.

How is it started?

The first UN peacekeeping operation—the United Nations Truce Supervision Organization (UNTSO), an observer mission, was established in 1948, in the Middle East.

Earlier in 1947, the United Nations adopted a plan to divide Palestine and create a Jewish and an Arab State. On May 15, 1948, the British administrative power formally ended its control over Palestine, and within 24 hours the State of Israel was proclaimed. Fierce hostilities broke out immediately between the Arab and Jewish communities. Count Bernadotte of Sweden, who was appointed by the United Nations to mediate the conflict, was able to negotiate a cease-fire. But as the hostilities continued and the number of Palestinian refugees fleeing Israel grew, the Security Council decided to create a Truce Commission to supervise the cease-fire. Count Bernadotte was to be assisted in this by a group of military observers. Unfortunately the Count was assassinated in the Israeli-held sector of Jerusalem on September 17, 1948. He was succeeded by Ralph Bunche of the United States, who took over as Acting Mediator. He directed the military observers and laid down the operation procedure.

What are the common features of peacekeeping operations?

While each UN peacekeeping operation is unique, all require the consent of parties involved in a dispute; none can be imposed unilateral or from outside; none involve military enforcement measures of coercive actions, except in the very limited context of self-defence or defence of civilian populations; all involve the deployment in the field of existing UN staff and of personnel (military and/or civilian) made available to the Secretary-General by  governments; all are under the operational command of the Secretary General of the UN; all are deployed to help control and resolve international conflicts or, increasingly, internal conflicts having an international dimension.

How does a peacekeeping mission start?

Peacekeeping operations are normally set up by the Security Council, the UN organ with primary responsibility for maintaining international peace and security. The Council decides the operation's size, its overall objectives and its time frame. As the UN has no military or civilian police force of its own, Member States decide whether to participate in a mission and, if so, what personnel and equipment they are willing to offer. Under the present structure, this can take considerable time for the actual forces to be authorized and reach their destination.

In some cases, peacekeepers have been sent to places where there was no peace to keep. In Sierra Leone while monitoring a peace agreement, contempt rather than cooperation was experienced by UN soldiers who were abducted; some were later killed. In Somalia, the parties repeatedly violated ceasefire agreements, and UN personnel became targets for murder, kidnapping and intimidation. Those who committed these crimes knew well that casualties can undermine support for a peacekeeping operation among the nations providing troops for it. Even in cases where there was a peace agreement, as in Angola and in Cambodia, peace-keepers have had to contend with recalcitrant rebel groups for whom was a profitable enterprise, since these groups controlled valuable export commodities, such as diamonds, drugs and timbers.

How do governments contribute to peacekeeping?

Contributions come in various forms both human and material. The soldiers and officers serving a UN peacekeeping operation are trained, selected and sent by their own countries. Besides the military troops, there are often civilian police officers, engineers to build roads, medical personnel, pilots, communications experts and many others. Military personnel, international civilian observers and local civilians from the area all work together in an operation.

Governments also contribute a wide range of components for the many functions of peacekeeping operations such as tents, portable structures for housing, hospitals or offices, furnishings and equipment, road transport utility aircraft and many others as well as services such as strategic sealift/airlift operations.

Task 2   Answer the following questions.

1. What is the objective of today's peace operations?

2. How many times was the technique of peacekeeping used in the UN's first 40 years?

3. How to define peacekeepers briefly?

4. What are the specific missions of peacekeepers?

5. What is the first UN peacekeeping operation?

6. What UN organ is authorized to set up peacekeeping operations?

7. Can you take examples to illustrate that peacekeepers are often in great danger?

Task 3   Complete the following translation tasks.

1. Chinese into English

1) 观察团通常包括非武装军事人员和文职人员,他们对停火协定的执行情况进行监督。

2) 维和部队由轻装部队构成,并配有装备齐全的步兵队伍。

3) 由于联合国本身没有军事或民事警察部队,因此,由其成员国决定是否参与某项任务,如若参加,该成员国还需确定派遣人员以及所需提供的装备。

4）各国政府所做的贡献包括人力、物力等多种形式。

5）参与联合国维和行动的士兵和军官均由本国培训、挑选及派遣。

2. English into Chinese

Most UN peacekeepers—often referred to as "**blue helmets**" because of the blue color helmets they wear while on duty—have been soldiers, volunteered by their Governments to apply military discipline and training to the task of restoring and maintaining peace: monitoring cease-fires, separating hostile forces and maintaining buffer zones. Civilian police officers, electoral observers, human rights monitors and other civilians have joined UN peacekeepers in recent years. Their tasks range from protecting and delivering humanitarian assistance, to helping former opponents carry out complicated peace agreements.

Task 4 Give an oral presentation in class on the following topics.

1. A Brief Description of the Common Features of Peacekeeping Operations

2. My Opinions toward Peacekeeping Forces

Part II Watching to Speak

Topic 1 UN Peacekeeping — Today

Task 1 Watch and tick the areas mentioned in the video clip.

Puji		Haiti	
Lebanon		Kosovo	
Darfur		Mali	
Syria		Liberia	
Timor-Leste		Kuwait	
Sudan		Libya	

Task 2 Watch the video again and fill in the blanks.

More than a (1)_____ other nations around the world, UN peacekeepers are in the front pages and on the (2)_____ working to bring peace to some of the world's most (3)_____ people. Never before has UN peacekeeping been as big as it is today; and never before has United Nations been asked to make such a broad (4) _____ to peace, (5) _____ and development. In societies that have (6) _____ through (7) _____. The United Nations has become the (8) _____ organization (9) _____ international (10) _____.

Task 3   What is peacekeeping according to Sir Brian Urquhart?

Task 4   Complete the information of the areas in which the UN peacekeepers are involved.

Today's efforts link peacekeeping to other areas of UN action like:

- _____ aid;
- the _____ of human rights;
- _____;
- building national _____;
- training the police;
- assisting the _____ systems;
- supporting _____.

Task 5   Watch the video and tick True (T) or False (F) about the women peacekeepers.

1. Women cannot be deployed as peacekeepers to fulfill peacekeeping missions.
   ☐ T ☐ F
2. Women peacekeepers are far from satisfied according to their performance in peacekeeping operations. ☐ T ☐ F
3. In all the conflict situations, more often than not, women have been more victimized compared with men. ☐ T ☐ F
4. In many situations women only play a minor role in rebuilding peace. ☐ T ☐ F
5. Women peacekeepers are only deployed in some societies, not worldwide. ☐ T ☐ F

Task 6   Watch the video clip and put the following sentences in order.

a) No infrastructure, no housing, no accommodation, no office space, no water or ablution facilities.

b) In many cases, peacekeeping missions come to places where there were absolutely nothing.

c) A world-class support system must be in place to back them.

d) All of these have to be built on the ground up.

e) Peacekeeping is routinely between the 20 th and 25 th largest aviation fleet in the world.

f) To be effective, today's blue helmets have to be organized.

Correct order: _____

Task 7   **How much does it cost for the UN to work for peace?**

Task 8   **What virtues are still required of UN peacekeepers?**

(1) _____, (2) _____, (3) _____, and (4) _____ that by working together we can make a better world.

Task 9   **Talk with your partner about UN peacekeepers' job. You may refer to the following phrases and sentence patterns.**

| security | international crises | conflict | vulnerable |
| essential | suffered through | corresponding to | to bring peace to |

In the course of pursuing peace, UN peacekeepers are always ready to ... (do sth.) to ... (who). Never before has UN peacekeeping been as ... (adjective) as it is today; and never before has the United Nation been ... (done) to ... (do sth.)

Topic 2   UN Peacekeeping — Before

Task 1   **Write down the key information about UN Charter.**

The UN Charter was signed (1) _____ (when) in (2) _____ (where) by (3) _____ (who).

Task 2   **Watch the video and repeat what Ralf Bunche said.**

Task 3   **Watch the video clip and answer the questions.**

What historical incident made it difficult for the UN Security Council to agree on matters of peace and security?	
When was the UN suddenly drawn into a full-scale international crisis?	
What's the full name of the organization of UN peacekeeping operation in the Middle East?	

Task 4 Complete the missing information on Cashmere.

Cashmere is a disputing territory between (1) _____ and (2) _____. The two countries agreed on a cease fire in the year of (3) _____.

Task 5 What big crisis other than Cashmere erupted in the Middle East?

Task 6 Present the principles provided by Secretary General Dag Hammarskjold.

The basic principles are as follows:
- The first principle is that the (1) _____ be ready to accept (2) _____ UN peacekeepers to help them resolve their (3) _____.
- Secondly, a (4) _____ must be in place.
- Thirdly, peacekeepers will not use force except in (5) _____.

Task 7 Watch for a second time and talk with your partner about the function of the three basic principles. You may use the following words.

| basis | remain | guide | carry out |
| include | peacekeeping mission | future operation | large operation |

Topic 3 Indian UN Peacekeepers

Task 1 Watch the video clip and discuss in your group what it is about.

Task 2 Watch again and fill in the blanks.

For the United Nations it's been a road well (1) _____, a-60-year journey (2) _____ the harsh terrain of global politics creating (3) _____ out of its success story. In these years, United Nations has successfully overcome (4) _____ and achieved (5) _____ with the (6) _____ and contribution of Member States with international peacekeeping being one of the most (7) _____ tasks.

Task 3 What remarks are given to Indian peacekeepers according to the clip?

What are their good virtues?	
How many Indians are involved?	
How many operations did they participate?	

Task 4 What kind of military man can be selected as Indian peacekeepers?

Only the best officers and soldiers with that attributes like (1)_____ will do for peace-keeping missions. (2)_____ must be clearly understood and adhered to.

Task 5 What's the objective of Indian peacekeepers?

Task 6 Why was peacekeeping not included in UN Charter?

Task 7 How is India valued in terms of its contribution to the UN peace-keeping operation?

It is because of (1)_____ and (2)_____ contribution towards peace that India's (3)_____ with UN have been strong and are becoming even stronger with each passing day. India is proud to remains (4)_____ and (5)_____ to the needs of world peace. It is always prepared to contribute selflessly and (6)_____ to UN peace (7)_____. In order to make the world a better and safer place in times to come.

Task 8 Watch for a second time and talk with your partner about how the UN official expresses his thanks to the sacrifice. You may refer to the following sentence pattern.

I want to thank... (who) for... (what) and for... (what else)... (who) have paid... (what) while participating in the UN peacekeeping operations. And we are very grateful for... (what)

Part III Scenario Simulation

Work in groups. Act out the following scenarios with the language you have learned in this unit.

Scenario 1 Discuss the one of the conflicts erupted in Middle East.

Instructions: Refer to video clip U9-2.1 and 9-2.2.

Scenario 2 Develop ideas on the sacrifices Indian peacekeepers have ever made.

Instructions: Refer to video clip U9-3.3.

New Words

1. helmet 头盔;钢盔
2. refugee 避难者,难民
3. assassinate 暗杀,行刺
4. coercive 强制的,强迫的
5. kidnap 绑架,劫持
6. violate 违反;妨碍;侵犯
7. undermine 破坏;侵蚀
8. observer 观察员
9. improvisation 临时组建的队伍
10. reconciliation 和解,调停
11. humanitarian 人道主义的
12. abduct 劫持

Military Terms

1. buffer zone 军事缓冲区
2. infantry 步兵;步兵部队
3. contingent 分遣队,小分队
4. deploy 部署,调集(部队或军事力量)
5. sealift 海上补给的
6. airlift 空中补给的

Toponymy

1. Palestine 巴勒斯坦
2. Israel 以色列
3. Jerusalem 耶路撒冷
4. Sierra Leone 塞拉利昂
5. Somalia 索马里
6. Angola 安哥拉
7. Cambodia 柬埔寨

Cultural Notes

1. The Charter of the United Nations 联合国宪章

The Charter of the United Nations is the foundational treaty of the United Nations. It entered into force on 24 October 1945, after being ratified by the five permanent members of the Security Council. As a charter, it is a constituent treaty, and all members are bound by its articles. Furthermore, Article 103 of the Charter states that obligations to the United Nations prevail over all other treaty obligations. Most countries in the world have now ratified the Charter.

2. The United Nations Truce Supervision Organization (UNTSO) 联合国停战监督组织

The United Nations Truce Supervision Organization is an organization founded on 29 May 1948 for peacekeeping in the Middle East. Its primary task was providing the military command structure to the peace keeping forces in the Middle East to enable the peace keepers to observe and maintain the cease-fire, and as may be necessary in assisting the parties to the Armistice Agreements in the supervision of the application and observance of the terms of those Agreements.

3. The United Nations Security Council 联合国安全理事会

The United Nations Security Council is one of the six principal organs of the United Nations and is charged with the maintenance of international peace and security. Its powers include the establishment of peacekeeping operations, the establishment of international sanctions, and the authorization of military action through Security Council resolutions; it is the only UN body with the authority to issue binding resolutions to member states. The Security Council held its first session on 17 January 1946.

4. Ralph Bunche 拉尔夫·本奇

Ralph Bunche (August 7, 1903 (disputed) or 1904-December 9, 1971) was an American political scientist, academic, and diplomat who received the 1950 Nobel Peace Prize for his late 1940s mediation in Palestine. He was the first African American and person of color to be so honored in the history of the prize. He was involved in the formation and administration of the United Nations. In 1963, he was awarded the Medal of Freedom by President John F. Kennedy.

Unit 10　National Defense

Synopsis

Do you want to know the latest defense policy of our country? Strengthening national defense is a strategic task in China's modernization drive, and a key guarantee for safeguarding China's security and unity as well as building a well-off society in an all-round way. As cadets, it's a must for us to learn some basic information about our country's defense policy. Unit 10, *National Defense*, introduces defense white paper in 2013.

Learning Objectives

1. to know the general information about China's defense policy
2. to learn to talk about the highlights on the White Paper with idiomatic expressions
3. to master the language to talk about China's national defense

Part I　Reading to Know

Task 1　Read the Text.

The Diversified Employment of China's Armed Forces

In today's world, peace and development are facing new opportunities and challenges. It is a historic mission entrusted by the era to people of all nations to firmly grasp the opportunities, jointly meet the challenges, cooperatively maintain security and collectively achieve development.

It is China's unshakable national commitment and strategic choice to take the road of peaceful development. China unswervingly pursues an independent foreign policy of peace and a national defense policy that is defensive in nature. China opposes any form of hegemonism or power politics, and does not interfere in the internal affairs of other countries. China will never seek hegemony or behave in a hegemonic manner, nor will it engage in military expansion. China advocates a new security concept featuring mutual trust, mutual benefit, equality and coordination, and pursues comprehensive security, common security and cooperative security.

It is a strategic task of China's modernization drive as well as a strong guarantee for

China's peaceful development to build a strong national defense and powerful armed forces which are commensurate with China's international standing and meet the needs of its security and development interests. China's armed forces act to meet the new requirements of China's national development and security strategies, follow the theoretical guidance of the Scientific Outlook on Development, speed up the transformation of the generating mode of combat effectiveness, build a system of modern military forces with Chinese characteristics, enhance military strategic guidance and diversify the ways of employing armed forces as the times require. China's armed forces provide security guarantee and strategic support for national development, and make due contributions to the maintenance of world peace and regional stability.

Fundamental Policies and Principles

The diversified employment of China's armed forces adheres to fundamental policies and principles as follows:

1. **Safeguarding national sovereignty, security and territorial integrity, and supporting the country's peaceful development.** It is the goal of China's efforts in strengthening its national defense and the sacred mission of its armed forces, as stipulated in the Constitution of the People's Republic of China and other relevant laws.

2. **Aiming to win local wars under the conditions of informationization and expanding and intensifying military preparedness.** China's armed forces firmly base their military preparedness on winning local wars under the conditions of informationization, make overall and coordinated plans to promote military preparedness in all strategic directions, intensify the joint employment of different services and arms, and enhance warfighting capabilities based on information systems.

3. **Formulating the concept of comprehensive security and effectively conducting military operations other than war (MOOTW).** China's armed forces adapt themselves to the new changes of security threats, and emphasize the employment of armed forces in peacetime.

4. **Deepening security cooperation and fulfilling international obligations.** China's armed forces are the initiator and facilitator of and participant in international security cooperation.

5. **Acting in accordance with laws, policies and disciplines.** China's armed forces observe the country's Constitution and other relevant laws, comply with the purposes and principles of the UN Charter, and maintain their commitment to employing troops and taking actions according to law.

Building and Development of China's Armed Forces

China's armed forces are composed of the People's Liberation Army (PLA), the People's Armed Police Force (PAPF) and the militia. They play a significant role in China's overall strategies of security and development, and shoulder the glorious mission and sacred duty of safeguarding national sovereignty, security and development interests.

The PLA Air Force (PLAAF) is China's mainstay for air operations, responsible for its territorial air security and maintaining a stable air defense posture nationwide. It is primarily composed of aviation, ground air defense, radar, airborne and electronic countermeasures (ECM) arms. In line with the strategic requirements of conducting both offensive and defensive operations, the PLAAF is strengthening the development of a combat force structure that focuses on reconnaissance and early warning, air strike, air and missile defense, and strategic projection. It is developing such advanced weaponry and equipment as new-generation fighters and new-type ground-to-air missiles and radar systems, improving its early warning, command and communications networks, and raising its strategic early warning, strategic deterrence and long-distance air strike capabilities. The PLAAF now has a total strength of 398,000 officers and men, and an air command in each of the seven Military Area Commands (MACs) of Shenyang, Beijing, Lanzhou, Jinan, Nanjing, Guangzhou and Chengdu. In addition, it commands one airborne corps. Under each air command are bases, aviation divisions (brigades), ground-to-air missile divisions (brigades), radar brigades and other units.

Defending National Sovereignty, Security and Territorial Integrity

The fundamental tasks of China's armed forces are consolidating national defense, resisting foreign aggression and defending the motherland. Responding to China's core security needs, the diversified employment of the armed forces aims to maintain peace, contain crises and win wars; safeguard border, coastal and territorial air security; strengthen combat-readiness and warfighting-oriented exercises and drills; readily respond to and resolutely deter any provocative action which undermines China's sovereignty, security and territorial integrity; and firmly safeguard China's core national interests.

Safeguarding Territorial Air Security

The PLAAF is the mainstay of national territorial air defense, and in accordance with the instructions of the CMC, the PLAA, PLAN and PAPF all undertake some territorial air defense responsibilities. In peacetime, the chain of command of China's air defense runs from the PLAAF headquarters through the air commands of the military area commands to air defense units. The PLAAF exercises unified command over all air defense components in accordance with the CMC's intent. China's air defense system is composed of six sub-systems of reconnaissance and surveillance, command and control, aerial defense, ground air defense, integrated support and civil air defense. China has established an air defense force system that integrates reconnaissance and early warning, resistance, counterattack and protection. For air situation awareness means, air detection radars and early warning aircraft are the mainstay, supplemented by technical and ECM reconnaissance. For resistance means, fighters, fighter-bombers, ground-to-air missiles and antiaircraft artillery troops are the mainstay, supplemented by the strengths from the PLAA air defense force, militia and reserves, as well as civil air defense. For integrated protection means, various protection works and strengths are the mainstay, supplemented by specialized technical protection forces.

The PLAAF organizes the following routine air defense tasks: reconnaissance and early warning units are tasked with monitoring air situations in China's territorial air space and surrounding areas and keeping abreast of air security threats. Command organs at all levels are tasked with assuming routine combat readiness duties with the capital as the core, and border and coastal areas as the key, and commanding air defense operations at all times. Routine air defense troops on combat duty are tasked with carrying out air vigilance and patrols at sea, conducting counter-reconnaissance in border areas and verifying abnormal and unidentified air situations within the territory. The air control system is tasked with monitoring, controlling and maintaining air traffic order so as to ensure flight safety.

Task 2　Answer the following questions.

1. What is the nature of China's national defense policy?

2. What is the responsibility of PLAAF?

3. What does the PLAAF's combat force structure focus on?

4. What are the fundamental tasks of China's armed forces?

5. What does the diversified employment of the armed forces aim to do?

6. What is China's air defense system composed of?

Task 3　Complete the following translation tasks.

1. Chinese into English

1) 走和平发展道路,是中国坚定不移的国家意志和战略抉择。

2) 不论经济发展到什么程度,中国都永远不称霸,永远不搞军事扩张。

3) 中国倡导互信、互利、平等、协作的新安全观,寻求实现综合安全、共同安全、合作安全。

4) 中国武装力量在国家安全和发展战略全局中具有重要地位和作用,肩负着维护国家主权、安全、发展利益的光荣使命和神圣职责。

5) 面对复杂多变的安全环境,人民解放军坚决履行新世纪新阶段历史使命。

2. English into Chinese

The fundamental tasks of China's armed forces are consolidating national defense, resisting foreign aggression and defending the motherland. Responding to China's core security needs, the diversified employment of the armed forces aims to maintain peace, contain crises and win wars; safeguard border, coastal and territorial air security; strengthen combat-readiness and warfighting-oriented exercises and drills; readily respond to and resolutely deter any provocative action which undermines China's sovereignty, security and territorial integrity; and firmly safeguard China's core national interests.

Task 4 Give an oral presentation in class on the following topics.

1. Brief Introduction of China's National Defense Policy from different perspectives, e. g. nature, aim and basic principles, etc.

2. Debate: China's military build-up, especially its budgets are routinely commented upon by many countries. Organize a debate on "Whether China's Defense Expenditure Has Remained at A Moderate Level" with the help of relevant information in Cultural Notes.

Part II Watching to Speak

Topic 1 China's National Defense in 2013

Task 1 Watch the video clip and tell your desk mate what it is about.

Task 2 Watch the video clip and fill in the blanks with related information.

1. The 2013 edition of China's National Defense White Paper is the (1)_____ defense paper since (2)_____, and the first one devoted to (3)_____ .

2. This White Paper provides a more detailed account of the (4)_____ of today's PLA.

3. The White Paper highlights the main theme, and provides a systematic introduction to the (5)_____ , (6)_____ and (7)_____ of the armed forces.

Task 3 Watch again and answer the question.

What are the new missions for China's military?
1) Speeding up its modernization with _____ and _____ ;
2) Increasing _____ ;
3) Expanding participation in _____ and _____ .

Task 4 Watch the video clip and fill in the form about the priorities for China's armed forces.

	Present work	Focus
The Army	moving towards greater mobility with	
The Navy	strengthening blue-water operations with _____	
The Air Force	developing _____ , with development in reconnaissance, _____ , and _____	Its Strategic Nuclear force is pushing the transformation towards _____ .

Task 5 According to Chen Zhou, Professor of Chinese Academy of Military Sciences, what is the relation between peaceful development and building a strong army?

Task 6 Watch the video clip and decide whether the following statements are True or False.

1. During the latest inspection, Chinese President Xi Jinping objected to the idea that soldiers integrate their personal goals with the aim of building a strong army. ☐ T ☐ F
2. Leaders in Beijing believe China faces complex and diverse security challenges in protecting its sovereignty. ☐ T ☐ F
3. China's National Defense White Paper usually focuses on a specific issue instead of giving a general overview of national defense. ☐ T ☐ F
4. The Chinese military disclosed the names of the joint corps of its army in 2010. ☐ T ☐ F

Task 7 Talk with your partner about China's National Defense in 2010. You may refer to the following sentence pattern.

China has released ... , titled... The PLA says it aims to ... , and indicates ... The White Paper also illustrates ...

Topic 2 Hightlights on the White Paper

Task 1 Watch the video clip and answer the question by filling the blanks.

In which aspects does the paper show the growing transparency of the PLA?
1) It discloses the _____ of the army, navy and air forces, about _____.
2) It discloses the army's _____, composed of _____ and _____, all under the _____.
3) Some of the _____ is written into the paper, including _____, _____ and the _____.

Task 2 Watch the video clip and decide whether the following statements are True or False.

1. There isn't much new information in the White Paper, and that's part of the reason this paper focuses on one theme — arms control and disarmament of the PLA. ☐ T ☐ F
2. Since the White Paper focuses only on one theme, the continuity of the defense policy is not so clear. ☐ T ☐ F
3. The Paper emphasizes the armed forces should remain vigilant in training in real combat, and points out the new roles of the navy in protecting maritime sovereignty.
   ☐ T ☐ F
4. The Paper stresses that China will change its defensive policy into offensive one in an active manner. This means the PLA is ready to fight back when attacked. ☐ T ☐ F

Task 3 Watch the video clip and answer the questions.

What does the paper reflect?	
What does the first chapter introduce?	
What does the new White Paper show?	

Task 4 Watch the video clip and tick the challenges and threats China faces mentioned in the video.

1. Provocative actions are taken by some neighboring countries to challenge its sovereignty. ☐
2. Some neighboring countries are making troubles over the issue of the Diaoyu Islands.
   ☐

3. The threats posed by "three forces" — terrorism, separatism and extremism, are on the rise. □
4. Some other countries are trying to form military alliances to destabilize regional peace. □
5. The "Taiwan independence" separatist forces and their activities are still the biggest threat to the peaceful development of cross-Straits relations. □
6. Confrontation in cyberspace and space has intensified. □

Task 5 Watch the video and fill in the blanks.

In order to build a strong army, the navy is speeding up its (1)_____ with an introduction of (2)_____ , to develop into a maritime power. The navy has gone beyond (3)_____ , testing its combat strength in (4)_____ . The white paper says the navy has deployed over (5)_____ in nearly 20 groups in (6)_____ over the past few years.

Task 6 Talk with your partner about the security threats and challenges China faces today. You may refer to the following phrases and sentence patterns.

territorial integrity   national unification   development interests
cross-Straits relations   the issues of subsistence and development security
the traditional and non-traditional threats to security

Today, China still faces ... and ... security threats and challenges. The issues of ... and ... are interwoven. Some country has ... On the issues concerning ... , some neighboring countries are ... , and ... is making trouble over the issue of ... The threats posed by ... are on the rise. ... is still the biggest threat to ...

Topic 3 Studio Interview

Task 1 Watch the video clip and tell your partner what they are talking about.

Task 2 Watch the video clip and answer the questions.

1. What is the main task of the 18 corps according to Captain Zhang Junshe, the Vice Prresident of the Naval Research Institute?
2. The white paper announces the 18 joint corps of the Chinese Army. What does this show?

Task 3　Watch the video clip and fill in the blanks.

China's nuclear policy: _____

Task 4　Talk with your partner about Chinese Air Force. You may refer to the following sentence patterns.

Chinese Air Force is . . . It is composed of . . . Its main task is . . .

Part III　Scenario Simulation

Work in groups. Act out the following scenarios with the language you have learned in this unit.

Scenario 1　Press Conference

Instructions: One acts as the spokesman of China's State Council Information Office and introduces China's National Defense policy in 2013, while the others act as journalists from different countries, raising questions related to the policy.

Scenario 2　Interview

Instructions: One of two acts as the host from CCTV. The other acts as a military expert. You may talk about the challenges and threats China faces today or put forward your own idea on China's defense policy.

Sample questions:

1) For the first time, the Chinese military has disclosed the names of the 18 combined corps of its Army. Would you say this reflects a growing transparency of the PLA?

2) The White Paper mentions that China is facing complex threats and challenges. Can you tell us more about those challenges?

New Words

1. entrust 委托,信托
2. unshakable 不可动摇的、坚定不移的
3. unswervingly 坚定不移地
4. hegemonism 霸权主义
5. interfere 干涉、介入
6. commensurate 相称的,同量的,同样大小的
7. diversify 使多样化

8. due 应付的
9. adhere 坚持
10. sovereignty 主权
11. territorial 领土的
12. integrity 完整
13. sacred 神圣的
14. stipulate 规定
15. preparedness 做好准备（尤指作战准备）
16. initiator 发起人,创始者
17. facilitator 促进者
18. comply 遵守
19. mainstay 支柱
20. deterrence 威慑
21. consolidating 巩固
22. aggression 侵略
23. deter 制止
24. provocative 挑衅的
25. undermine 破坏,危害
26. abreast 并肩地,并排地
27. vigilance 警戒
28. verify 核实,查证
29. escort 护卫,护航
30. multi-dimensional 多维的
31. vessel 船,舰
32. vigilant 警惕的,警醒的
33. maritime 海事的,沿海的
34. alliance 联盟,同盟
35. destabilize 使动摇
36. frontier 边界
37. transparency 透明;透明化

Military Terms

1. strategic projection 战略投送
2. combat-readiness 战备
3. antiaircraft artillery troops 高炮部队
4. reserve 预备役
5. blue water training 远海训练

6. combat force structure 作战力量体系
7. counterattack 反击,反攻
8. precision strikes 精确打击
9. confrontation 对抗
10. deployment 调度;部署
11. corps 集团军
12. Central Military Commission (CMC) 中央军事委员会

Cultural Notes
1. militia 民兵
The militia is an armed organization composed of the people not released from their regular work. As an assistant force of the PLA, the militia is tasked with participating in the socialist modernization drive, performing combat readiness support and defensive operations, helping maintain social order and participating in emergency rescue and disaster relief operations.

2. Defense Policy in 2010 2010 年国防政策
China pursues a national defense policy which is purely defensive in nature. China places the protection of national sovereignty, security, territorial integrity, safeguarding of the interests of national development, and the interests of the Chinese people above all else. China endeavors to build a fortified national defense and strong military forces compatible with national security and development interests, and enrich the country and strengthen the military while building a moderately prosperous society in all aspects.